HEINZ FIELD COOKBOOK

RECIPES FOR SAVORING THE
GAME FROM THE SIDELINES

Heinz Field Cookbook
Recipes for Savoring the Game from the Sidelines

H.J. Heinz Company
P.O. Box 57
Pittsburgh PA 15230-0057 USA

All registered trademarks of H.J. Heinz Company are authorized for use herein.
Hormel® is a registered trademark of Hormel Foods Corporation.
Kahlúa® Liqueur is a registered trademark of Allied Domecq Spirits USA.
Oreo® and Cheez Whiz® are registered trademarks of Kraft Foods, Inc.
Old Bay® Seasoning is a registered trademark of McCormick & Co., Inc.

Published by:
Levine Communications
428 Stratton Lane
Pittsburgh, PA 15206

To order copies, contact:
A Glimmer of Hope
1-800-GLIMPIN (454-6746)
www.breastcure.com

Manufactured by Favorite Recipes® Press
An imprint of

2451 Atrium Way
Nashville, Tennessee 37214

ISBN: 0-9742658-0-2
Library of Congress Control Number: 2003108975

Printed in the United States of America
First Printing: August, 2003   hardbound edition   12,500 copies

HEINZ FIELD
COOKBOOK

RECIPES FOR SAVORING THE GAME FROM THE SIDELINES

A Message from H.J. Heinz Company

Dear Friends,

From time to time we each are presented with an opportunity to do something truly special for other people. That opportunity came to Heinz when *A Glimmer of Hope* approached us to create a cookbook to raise money for breast cancer research.

With our company's name adorning Heinz Field and our Heinz Red Zone Recipes for tailgating parties, Heinz enjoys an established connection with football. Therefore, we just couldn't resist the chance to tackle this project!

This cookbook contains some of the best recipes of current and former Pittsburgh Steelers players, coaches, and their wives, along with some interesting tidbits about what makes each recipe so personally appealing. We've also added some terrific recipes from five accomplished chefs that are sure to add variety to your culinary 'playbook'.

Proceeds from the sale of each cookbook go to *A Glimmer of Hope*. By supporting the foundation's funding of breast cancer research, you'll give thousands of women and their families more than just a "glimmer" of hope for more effective treatments, as well as helping to find an eventual cure for this terrible disease.

We hope you enjoy these recipes and we thank you for supporting *A Glimmer of Hope*.

With our gratitude,

William R. Johnson, Chairman, President and CEO, with his wife, Susie

Bill and Susie Johnson

ACKNOWLEDGEMENTS

Heartfelt thanks to the Rooney family, the Pittsburgh Steelers organization and management, current and former Steelers players, wives, and coaches who have supported the idea of this book from the very beginning. Many of these dedicated, community-minded people have contributed favorite family recipes to the Heinz Field Cookbook. You'll find their recipes flagged by a black football helmet and the name of the contributor.

Each of the Steelers recipes was tested by Rania Harris and the professional chefs of Rania's Catering in Mt. Lebanon, Pennsylvania to ensure their success in your kitchen. The cookbook also contains a number of recipes donated by Rania in support of the book's mission to raise funds for research into a cure for breast cancer.

This cookbook owes its mouth-watering appeal to the superb photographers and stylists whose work illuminates its pages:

Photographers: John Sanderson, Sanderson Studio (cover, chapter openers, and desserts) and Michael Ray, Michael Ray Photography
Photo Assistants: Ed Labuda and R. Alan Adams
Food Stylist: Shui Ziegler with Ana Kelly, Food Assistant
Prop Stylist: Robert Ziegler

Thanks to Kelly McKenzie, principal - Group 2 Design, and the marvelous imagination and discerning eye of his design and layout team, Linda DeLaney and Ron Grice, whose graphic design sensibilities and talents have made this book so beautiful to page through and so reader-friendly to use.

Last, but not least, thanks jointly to Robin Teets, Senior Communication Manager, who served as the absolutely unflappable Heinz liaison on the project and to Karen Levine – freelance project manager, editor and writer – who quarterbacked the team that produced this book and brought in the winning touchdown against a mighty opponent: an aggressive schedule as tight as a two-minute warning.

Our gratitude goes to each of you for your commitment to the success of this project. We trust the cookbook will score big for *A Glimmer of Hope* in its efforts to raise funds for breast cancer research and, most importantly, to find a cure.

Debora S. Foster
Director, Corporate Communications
H.J. Heinz Company

A GLIMMER OF HOPE

To Our Supporters,

Carol Jo Weiss Friedman and I were best friends for 12 years. We lived through each other's marriages, the births of our children, career decisions, and all the things that make a lasting friendship. When Carol Jo died of breast cancer in 1990, I was devastated by the loss and resolved to make a difference by doing something in my friend's memory. That resolve led me to form *A Glimmer of Hope* – an organization dedicated to raising funds for breast cancer research.

Julie Faneca, Alan Faneca and Diana Napper

The statistics are horrifying. More than 180,000 women are diagnosed with breast cancer each year. One out of eight women will develop breast cancer in her lifetime. So much research is still needed to develop ever more effective treatments for women who develop the disease and to continue to search aggressively for a cure.

The H.J. Heinz Company generously underwrote the cost of creating the Heinz Field Cookbook as a fundraiser to benefit *A Glimmer of Hope's* charitable mission. Proceeds from the sale of every cookbook will go to the Magee-Womens Health Foundation Glimmer of Hope Fund to support the efforts of physicians and research scientists at Magee-Womens Research Institute as well as to other breast cancer research centers across the country. These dedicated investigators are revolutionizing the treatment and care of women with breast cancer.

Thank you for helping to make their work possible by purchasing this cookbook. Hopefully, one day soon, they will also find a cure.

Sincerely,

Diana Napper

Diana Napper, Founder
A Glimmer of Hope
1-800-GLIMPIN (454-6746)
www.breastcure.com

CONTENTS

TAILGATE TEMPTATIONS

PRE-GAME WARM-UPS

CONTENTS (CONTINUED)

HALFTIME HIGHLIGHTS

TWO-MINUTE WARNING

VICTORY CELEBRATIONS

TAILGATE TEMPTATIONS

FIRE UP your team with a combination of great dishes you can prepare in advance or grill at the game. These gridiron favorites will keep your fans coming back for more, game after game, all season long.

CARIBBEAN
SALSA

MAKES 2 QUARTS

2 (28-ounce) cans
diced tomatoes in juice

1 cup (⅜-inch pieces) mango

1 cup (⅜-inch pieces) red onion

¾ cup (¼-inch pieces)
Anaheim green chiles

½ cup (¼-inch pieces)
red bell pepper

½ cup (¼-inch pieces)
yellow bell pepper

¼ cup chopped fresh cilantro

1 tablespoon Caribbean
jerk seasoning

1 tablespoon lime juice

1 tablespoon olive oil

½ teaspoon salt

Combine the undrained tomatoes, mango, onion, chiles, bell peppers, cilantro, jerk seasoning, lime juice, olive oil and salt in a 3-quart container and mix well. Chill, covered, for 2 to 3 hours before serving to blend the flavors. Serve as a dip for tortilla chips or as a topping or condiment with hot or cold Caribbean foods, beef, chicken or seafood.

CHILI
SALSA

MAKES ABOUT 2 CUPS

1 (12-ounce) bottle
Heinz Chili Sauce

½ cup finely chopped
green bell pepper

½ cup finely chopped
yellow or red bell pepper

½ cup finely chopped onion

1 to 2 teaspoons
minced fresh cilantro

Combine the Heinz Chili Sauce, bell peppers, onion and cilantro in a medium bowl and mix well. Store in the refrigerator. Serve as a dip for tortilla chips or with grilled chicken, beef or fish.

PLAYBOOK

Heinz Field is home
to both the
Pittsburgh Steelers
and the University of
Pittsburgh Panthers.
In an interesting
coincidence,
American college
football and
the Heinz company
both got their
start in 1869.

CHILI

MAKES 8 SERVINGS

From Aaron Smith

"I love it when my wife, Jaimie, has a bowl of her special chili waiting for me after a long, hard, cold practice during the fall."

AARON SMITH

1 cup chopped onion
½ green bell pepper, chopped
1 cup chopped celery
2 tablespoons vegetable oil
1 pound ground beef
or ground turkey
2 (15-ounce) cans
diced tomatoes
¼ cup chili powder
2 tablespoons cold water
2 teaspoons sugar
1 teaspoon garlic powder
2 teaspoons cumin
1½ teaspoons salt
1 (15-ounce) can kidney beans
1 (15-ounce) can pinto beans
1 (15-ounce) can black beans

Sauté the onion, bell pepper and celery in the oil in a skillet. Add the ground beef and cook until brown and crumbly, stirring frequently; drain. Combine the ground beef mixture with the tomatoes in a large saucepan. Blend the chili powder with the water in a cup and add to the saucepan. Stir in the sugar, garlic powder, cumin and salt and mix well. Bring to a boil and reduce the heat. Simmer for 1 hour. Drain the beans and add to the saucepan. Cook until heated through.

SENSATIONAL
SLOPPY JOES

MAKES 6 SANDWICHES

1 pound ground turkey
or ground beef

1 large onion, chopped

1 cup Heinz Tomato Ketchup

1 tablespoon Heinz
Worcestershire Sauce

¼ cup water

¼ teaspoon salt

⅛ teaspoon pepper

6 sandwich buns

Brown the ground turkey or ground beef with the
onion in a nonstick skillet, stirring until the turkey
is crumbly; drain. Stir in the Heinz Tomato Ketchup,
Heinz Worcestershire Sauce, water, salt and pepper.
Simmer for 12 to 15 minutes or to the desired
degree of doneness, stirring occasionally. Serve in
the sandwich buns.

STEWED BEEF
WITH TOMATOES

MAKES 6 SERVINGS

¼ cup vegetable oil

2 garlic cloves, crushed

4 slices gingerroot

2 pounds beef brisket, cut into 1-inch cubes

¼ cup Heinz Tomato Ketchup

2 tablespoons rice wine or dry sherry

⅔ cup soy sauce

2 tablespoons sugar

⅔ cup water

2 tomatoes, sliced

Heat the oil in a large saucepan over high heat for 1 minute. Add the garlic and gingerroot and stir-fry for 30 seconds or until golden brown. Add the beef and stir-fry until light brown. Add the Heinz Tomato Ketchup, wine, soy sauce and sugar and mix well. Cook, covered, for 5 minutes. Add the water and bring to a boil. Reduce the heat to low and simmer for 1½ hours. Stir in the tomatoes and simmer for 30 minutes longer or until the beef is very tender.

BEEF AND BEAN BURRITOS

MAKES 8 BURRITOS

8 ounces lean ground beef
1 cup Heinz Tomato Ketchup
1 cup prepared tomato salsa
1 (15-ounce) can pinto beans
8 flour tortillas
1½ cups shredded
Cheddar cheese
Shredded lettuce

Brown the ground beef in a large skillet, stirring until crumbly; drain. Add the Heinz Tomato Ketchup, salsa and pinto beans. Cook until heated through. Spoon about ½ cup of the mixture down the center of each tortilla and sprinkle each with 2 tablespoons of the cheese. Fold the tortillas to enclose the filling. Line serving plates with lettuce and place the burritos seam side down on the lettuce. Top with the remaining cheese and additional salsa if desired.

PLAYBOOK

To "pour on" the excitement during Pittsburgh Steelers and University of Pittsburgh Panthers home games, the H.J. Heinz Company has had two giant Heinz Ketchup bottles affixed to the stadium's Jumbotron, one on each side. The ketchup bottles are:

Thirty-five feet long
Nine feet high
Six feet deep
Weigh eight thousand pounds each

TURKEY TD BURGERS
WITH BARBECUED RED ONIONS

MAKES 4 SERVINGS

CHIPOTLE MAYONNAISE
Juice of ½ lime
½ cup mayonnaise
1 tablespoon pureed canned chipotle chile in adobo sauce, or to taste
1 teaspoon sugar

TURKEY BURGERS AND BARBECUED RED ONIONS
1½ pounds ground turkey
Kosher salt and freshly ground pepper to taste
4 (½-inch) slices red onion
Jack Daniel's® Sizzling Smokehouse Blend™ Grilling Sauce
Sliced Pepper Jack cheese
4 sesame seed hamburger buns, toasted
Sliced avocado (optional)

FOR THE MAYONNAISE, combine the lime juice, mayonnaise, pureed chipotle chile and sugar in a small bowl and mix well. Let stand for 30 minutes to blend the flavors.

FOR THE BURGERS AND ONIONS, season the ground turkey with kosher salt and pepper and mix gently. Shape into 4 patties ¾-inch thick. Spray with non-stick cooking spray to prevent their sticking to the grill.

Place the onion slices on the grill and brush with Jack Daniel's Sizzling Smokehouse Blend Grilling Sauce. Grill for 8 minutes or until tender, turning frequently and brushing with additional sauce.

Grill the burgers for 5 minutes, then turn and top with the cheese. Grill for 4 to 5 minutes longer or to 160°F on a meat thermometer. Remove to the hamburger buns and top with the mayonnaise, grilled onions and avocado slices.

KICKIN' CHICKEN
SANDWICHES

MAKES 4 SERVINGS

1 cup mayonnaise

½ cup Classico® di Genova Traditional Basil Pesto Sauce & Spread

4 boneless skinless chicken breasts

Olive oil

Salt and pepper to taste

4 (4 x 4-inch) focaccia squares

8 slices fresh mozzarella cheese

4 canned artichoke hearts, drained and sliced thin

2 plum tomatoes, sliced thin

2 cups mixed field greens

Combine the mayonnaise and Classico di Genova Traditional Basil Pesto Sauce & Spread in a small bowl and whisk to blend well.

Brush the chicken lightly with olive oil and season with salt and pepper. Grill over medium-high heat for 5 minutes on each side or until cooked through. Remove to a cutting board and cool slightly. Cut diagonally into ½-inch slices.

Split the focaccia squares horizontally and spread the cut surfaces with the mayonnaise and pesto mixture. Layer the chicken, mozzarella cheese, artichoke hearts, tomatoes and mixed greens on the bottom halves of the bread and top with the remaining halves.

SOUTHWESTERN
PASTA SALAD

MAKES 5 SERVINGS

SOUTHWESTERN DRESSING
1 cup Heinz Tomato Ketchup
¼ cup mayonnaise
1 tablespoon taco seasoning mix
⅓ cup milk

SALAD
3 cups uncooked rotini
1 (15-ounce) can
kidney beans, drained
1 (15-ounce) can corn
1 tomato, chopped
½ cup chopped red
or green bell pepper
½ cup sliced celery
½ cup sliced green onions
½ cup sliced black
or green olives
Leaf lettuce
Shredded Cheddar cheese

FOR THE DRESSING, combine the Heinz Tomato Ketchup, mayonnaise and taco seasoning mix in a bowl and mix well. Stir in the milk. Store in the refrigerator.

FOR THE SALAD, cook the pasta using the package directions; rinse and drain. Chill in the refrigerator. Combine the pasta, kidney beans, undrained corn, tomato, bell pepper, celery, green onions and olives in a large bowl and mix gently. Add the dressing and toss gently to mix. Spoon onto lettuce-lined plates and sprinkle each serving with Cheddar cheese.

(MAKE NO) MIS-STEAKS
WITH TOMATO SALAD

MAKES 6 SERVINGS

STEAKS

1 cup olive oil

⅓ cup fresh lemon juice

⅓ cup chopped fresh rosemary

Freshly ground pepper to taste

6 (12-ounce) T-bone steaks, about 1-inch thick

Salt to taste

Jack Daniel's® Sizzling Smokehouse Blend™ Grilling Sauce

TOMATO SALAD

6 large tomatoes, sliced

2 teaspoons Heinz Balsamic Vinegar

5 teaspoons olive oil

Salt and pepper to taste

½ cup kalamata olive halves

½ cup crumbled blue cheese

2 tablespoons drained capers

4 anchovies, drained and chopped (optional)

FOR THE STEAKS, combine the olive oil, lemon juice, rosemary and a generous amount of pepper in a large baking dish and mix well. Add the steaks and turn to coat well. Marinate, covered, in the refrigerator for 4 to 6 hours. Drain, discarding the marinade. Sprinkle the steaks with salt. Grill over medium-high heat for 5 minutes on each side or to the desired degree of doneness, basting constantly with Jack Daniel's Sizzling Smokehouse Blend Grilling Sauce.

FOR THE SALAD, arrange the sliced tomatoes on a large platter. Drizzle with the Heinz Balsamic Vinegar and olive oil. Season lightly with salt and generously with pepper. Top with the olives, blue cheese, capers and anchovies. Garnish with basil leaves and serve with the steaks.

ROCK 'EM SOCK 'EM
SUNDAY STEAKS

MAKES 4 SERVINGS

4 (8-ounce) filets mignon

2 cups tomato juice

2 tablespoons Heinz
Worcestershire Sauce

¼ cup pepper vodka

2 tablespoons fresh lime juice

1 tablespoon squeezed
prepared white horseradish

Hot sauce to taste

½ teaspoon celery salt

Freshly ground pepper to taste

Ore-Ida® Zesties!
French Fried Potatoes

Heinz Kick'rs™
Hot & Spicy Flavored Ketchup

Arrange the steaks in a shallow dish. Combine the tomato juice, Heinz Worcestershire Sauce, vodka, lime juice, horseradish, hot sauce, celery salt and pepper in a bowl and whisk to mix well. Pour over the steaks, turning to coat well. Marinate in the refrigerator for 1 to 2 hours, turning the steaks several times. Drain, discarding the marinade. Grill the steaks over high heat for 4 to 6 minutes on each side for medium-rare or to the desired degree of doneness. Remove to a serving platter.

Serve with Ore-Ida Zesties! French Fried Potatoes and Heinz Kick'rs Hot & Spicy Flavored Ketchup to kick up the fries!

PLAYBOOK

When the Steelers or the Panthers enter the Heinz Red Zone – the area between the 20-yard line and the goal – the two Heinz Ketchup bottles tilt downward, the bottle caps flip up, and red "LEDs," or light-emitting diodes, flow downward simulating ketchup pouring out of a bottle. The pouring action triggers animation on the Jumbotron that encourages fan participation.

SUPER STEELERS STEAKS
WITH CHIPOTLE BARBECUE SAUCE

MAKES 6 SERVINGS

CHIPOTLE RED CHILE PASTE

4 ancho chiles, seeded

4 dried Mexican chiles, seeded

3 cups chicken broth

½ white onion, chopped

3 garlic cloves, minced

2 chipotle chiles, seeded

**CHIPOTLE BARBECUE
SAUCE AND STEAK**

1 tablespoon vegetable oil

2 cups chopped yellow onions

7 garlic cloves, minced

1 cup Heinz Tomato Ketchup

¼ cup Heinz
Apple Cider Vinegar

½ cup Heinz
Worcestershire Sauce

½ cup strong brewed coffee

¼ cup fresh lemon juice

⅓ cup packed brown sugar

2 teaspoons Heinz
Spicy Brown Mustard

2 teaspoons kosher salt

6 (8- to 10-ounce)
rib-eye steaks

FOR THE CHILE PASTE, combine the ancho chiles, dried Mexican chiles and chicken stock in a large saucepan. Add the onion and garlic. Bring to a boil over high heat. Reduce the heat and simmer for 15 minutes or until the peppers soften. Combine the mixture with the chipotle chiles in a blender and begin to process at low speed, increasing the speed as the mixture thickens. The mixture should measure about 3 cups. Remove 1 cup to use in the Chipotle Barbecue Sauce and store the remaining sauce in the refrigerator.

FOR THE SAUCE AND STEAK, heat the oil in a large heavy saucepan over medium heat and add the onions and garlic. Sauté until the vegetables begin to become tender. Add the Heinz Tomato Ketchup and the reserved 1 cup chile paste and sauté for 4 minutes. Add the Heinz Apple Cider Vinegar, Heinz Worcestershire Sauce, coffee, lemon juice, brown sugar, Heinz Spicy Brown Mustard and kosher salt and mix well. Simmer for 30 to 40 minutes or until thickened to the desired consistency, stirring frequently to prevent scorching. Cool the sauce to room temperature and process in a blender until pureed. Store in the refrigerator.

Brush the steaks lightly with the sauce. Grill to the desired degree of doneness. Bring the remaining sauce to a boil to serve with the steaks.

STRAWBERRY
SPINACH SALAD

MAKES 8 SERVINGS

From Janis and Kevin Colbert

SALAD DRESSING
⅓ cup vegetable oil

⅓ cup Heinz
Apple Cider Vinegar

¼ teaspoon Heinz
Worcestershire Sauce

1 tablespoon sugar

2 teaspoons minced
green onions

½ teaspoon paprika

Salt and pepper to taste

SALAD
2 tablespoons sesame seeds

1½ pounds fresh spinach, torn

2 cups strawberry halves

FOR THE DRESSING, combine the oil, Heinz Apple Cider Vinegar, Heinz Worcestershire Sauce, sugar, green onions, paprika, salt and pepper in a bowl and mix well.

FOR THE SALAD, sprinkle the sesame seeds in a small skillet. Toast over medium heat until golden brown, stirring to toast evenly. Combine with the spinach and strawberries in a large salad bowl. Add the salad dressing and toss gently to coat well. Serve immediately.

> "This is a family favorite that Janis makes on a hot summer day. It's great after a long day in the heat at training camp."
>
> **KEVIN COLBERT**

BARBECUED RIBS
WITH 3 HEINZ SAUCES

MAKES 4 SERVINGS

**4 pounds pork back ribs
or side ribs**

Chopped gingerroot to taste

¼ cup Heinz Tomato Ketchup

¼ cup Heinz 57 Sauce

**¼ cup Heinz
Worcestershire Sauce**

¼ cup dark soy sauce

¼ cup white wine or vermouth

½ teaspoon sesame oil

2 tablespoons cornstarch

1 tablespoon minced garlic

1 tablespoon chopped gingerroot

1 tablespoon sugar

**2 tablespoons chopped
green onions**

1½ teaspoons pepper

Cut the ribs into single-rib portions. Combine with water to cover and a generous amount of gingerroot in a large saucepan. Bring to a boil and cook for 30 minutes or until the ribs are tender; drain and cool the ribs. Combine the Heinz Tomato Ketchup, Heinz 57 Sauce, Heinz Worcestershire Sauce, soy sauce, wine, sesame oil, cornstarch, garlic, 1 tablespoon gingerroot, sugar, green onions and pepper in a bowl and mix well. Add the ribs and marinate in the refrigerator for 30 minutes or longer. Grill the ribs to the desired degree of doneness.

EZ Marinader™ Grilled
CHICKEN BREASTS

MAKES 4 SERVINGS

1 medium pineapple

1 medium red onion

1 package **EZ Marinader™**
Mr. Yoshida's® Teriyaki Flavor

4 (6-ounce) boneless
skinless chicken breasts

Cut the top off the pineapple and peel if desired. Cut the pineapple into 4 thick slices and cut each slice into halves, discarding the core. Cut the onion into 4 thick slices. Combine the pineapple and onion in the bag of EZ Marinader Mr. Yoshida's Teriyaki Flavor and seal the bag. Marinate in the refrigerator for 15 minutes, turning the bag occasionally to marinate evenly. Remove the pineapple and onion from the bag; cover and set aside. Place the chicken in the Marinader bag and reseal the bag. Marinate in the refrigerator for 30 minutes, turning the bag occasionally to marinate evenly.

Drain the chicken, discarding the marinade. Grill the chicken over medium heat for 4 to 6 minutes. Turn the chicken over and add the pineapple and onion to the grill. Grill for 4 to 6 minutes longer or until the chicken is cooked through, turning the pineapple and onion once.

CHICKEN
KICKOFF KABOBS

MAKES 4 SERVINGS

1 pound boneless
skinless chicken breasts,
cut into 1-inch pieces

1 green bell pepper,
cut into 1-inch pieces

1 red bell pepper,
cut into 1-inch pieces

1 fresh pineapple, cut into
chunks, or 1 (8-ounce) can
pineapple chunks, drained

½ cup Jack Daniel's®
Original No.7 Barbecue Recipe™
Grilling Sauce

¼ cup orange marmalade

Thread the chicken, green pepper, red pepper and pineapple alternately onto skewers until all ingredients are used. Combine the Jack Daniel's Original No.7 Barbecue Recipe Grilling Sauce and orange marmalade in a small bowl and mix well. Brush the mixture over the kabobs. Grill over medium coals for 15 minutes or until the chicken is cooked through, turning and brushing with additional sauce as needed.

COUNTRY-STYLE
RIBS

MAKES 4 SERVINGS

2 pounds pork ribs

1 (12-ounce) bottle
Heinz Chili Sauce

1 tablespoon
Heinz Worcestershire Sauce

1 tablespoon
Heinz Yellow Mustard

2 tablespoons lemon juice

2 tablespoons chopped onion

1 garlic clove, minced

1 tablespoon brown sugar

¼ teaspoon salt

Cut the ribs into serving portions and place in a
9 x 13-inch baking dish. Combine the Heinz Chili
Sauce, Heinz Worcestershire Sauce, Heinz Yellow
Mustard, lemon juice, onion, garlic, brown sugar
and salt in a bowl and mix well. Pour over the ribs,
turning to coat well. Bake, covered with foil, at
350°F for 1 hour or until tender, basting occasionally.
You may brush the ribs with the sauce and grill or
broil, uncovered, for 5 minutes on each side to brown
if desired. You may prepare the dish in advance and
store in the refrigerator until baking time.

HOT AND SWEET
BARBECUE SAUCE

MAKES 2⅔ CUPS

1 (14-ounce) bottle Heinz
Tomato Ketchup, about 1⅓ cups

¼ cup Heinz Apple Cider Vinegar

2 tablespoons Heinz 57 Sauce
or Heinz Worcestershire Sauce

1 (10- to 12-ounce) jar
orange marmalade

1 to 2 teaspoons chili powder

Combine the Heinz Tomato Ketchup, Heinz Apple
Cider Vinegar, Heinz 57 Sauce, orange marmalade
and chili powder in a small saucepan and mix well.
Cook over low heat until heated through and blended.
Use to brush on chicken, pork or beef during the last
5 to 10 minutes of grilling time. Bring any remaining
sauce to a boil to serve with the meat.

OYSTER SAUCE
BABY BACK RIBS

MAKES 4 TO 6 SERVINGS

From Tondi von Oelhoffen

4 racks baby back ribs
3 tablespoons crushed gingerroot
⅓ cup oyster sauce
1 cup Heinz Tomato Ketchup
¾ cup packed brown sugar
¾ cup soy sauce

Combine the ribs with the gingerroot and water to cover in a large saucepan. Bring to a boil and reduce the heat. Simmer for 45 to 60 minutes or until the ribs are tender; drain. Combine the oyster sauce, Heinz Tomato Ketchup, brown sugar and soy sauce in a large shallow dish and mix well. Add the ribs to the dish, turning to coat well. Marinate in the refrigerator for 8 hours or longer. Remove the ribs from the marinade and place on a grill. Grill until done to taste.

"This is my father's specialty and it's one of my family's favorite dishes. Once a year, our family goes to Hawaii to visit my family and they know whoever makes the ribs is the family member we'll visit first."

KIMO
VON OELHOFFEN

GRILLED
PORTERHOUSE STEAKS

MAKES 4 SERVINGS

**4 (1-inch-thick) Porterhouse
steaks or T-bone steaks**

**1 package EZ Marinader™
Jack Daniel's® Mesquite Flavor**

Place the steaks in the bag of EZ Marinader Jack Daniel's Mesquite Flavor and seal the bag. Marinate in the refrigerator for 20 to 30 minutes, turning the bag occasionally to marinate evenly. Remove from the bag and grill over medium-high heat for 8 to 12 minutes or to desired degree of doneness, turning halfway through the grilling process. Serve with grilled vegetables.

Easy
Jambalaya

MAKES 4 SERVINGS

½ cup chopped onion
⅓ cup chopped green bell pepper
⅓ cup chopped red bell pepper
2 garlic cloves, minced
1 tablespoon vegetable oil
1½ cups rice, cooked
1 cup chicken broth
½ cup Heinz Tomato Ketchup
½ teaspoon hot pepper sauce
1 pound shrimp,
peeled and deveined
2 tablespoons chopped parsley

Sauté the onion, bell peppers and garlic in the oil in a large saucepan until tender. Stir in the rice, chicken broth, Heinz Tomato Ketchup and hot pepper sauce. Simmer, covered, for 5 minutes. Add the shrimp and parsley. Cook, uncovered, for 4 to 5 minutes longer or until the shrimp are pink and cooked through, stirring once.

GOOD OL' GRILLED
PORK CHOPS

MAKES 4 SERVINGS

SPICE RUB AND PORK CHOPS

3 tablespoons paprika

2 tablespoons brown sugar

2 tablespoons ground cumin

1 tablespoon kosher salt

2 tablespoons
freshly ground pepper

4 (12-ounce) rib pork chops,
about 1½-inches thick

BARBECUE SAUCE

2 cups Jack Daniel's®
Tennessee Hickory Mesquite™
Grilling Sauce

5 fresh or frozen peaches,
chopped

½ cup orange juice

⅓ cup packed brown sugar

FOR THE SPICE RUB AND PORK CHOPS, combine the paprika, brown sugar, cumin, kosher salt and pepper in a small bowl and mix well. Rub into both sides of the pork chops and let stand while preparing the barbecue sauce.

FOR THE BARBECUE SAUCE, combine the Jack Daniel's Tennessee Hickory Mesquite Grilling Sauce, peaches, orange juice and brown sugar in a saucepan. Bring to a boil and reduce the heat. Simmer for 15 minutes or until slightly thickened, stirring occasionally. Process in a blender or food processor until smooth. Remove ¼ cup of the sauce for basting the pork chops and reserve the remaining sauce to serve with the pork chops.

TO GRILL THE PORK CHOPS, place on the grill and grill for 8 to 10 minutes on each side or until cooked through, basting with ¼ cup barbecue sauce during the last 30 seconds of grilling time on each side. Serve with the reserved barbecue sauce.

ORANGE
ALMOND SAUCE

MAKES 1½ CUPS

1 (12-ounce) jar
sweet orange marmalade
¼ cup **Heinz 57 Sauce**
2 tablespoons minced onion
2 teaspoons lemon juice
1 teaspoon soy sauce
¼ teaspoon ground ginger
⅛ teaspoon red pepper
⅛ teaspoon allspice
¼ cup sliced almonds

Combine the orange marmalade, Heinz 57 Sauce, onion, lemon juice, soy sauce, ginger, red pepper and allspice in a small saucepan. Cook over medium-low heat for 10 minutes or until heated through, stirring occasionally. Stir in the almonds. Serve over pork, ham, chicken or duck.

PLAYBOOK

The two Heinz Field
Ketchup bottles
weigh a total
of 16,000 pounds –
the equivalent of
fifty-three
300-pound linemen.

Honey 'N' Spice
Chicken Kabobs

MAKES 4 SERVINGS

PLAYBOOK

If the scoreboard's Heinz Ketchup bottles were filled with Heinz Ketchup, they would contain 1,664,000 fluid ounces each. That's enough to pour on approximately 3.2 million hotdogs or give each person seated at Heinz Field at least one 14-ounce bottle of ketchup to take home.

1 medium green bell pepper
4 boneless skinless chicken breasts
1 (16-ounce) can pineapple chunks
½ cup Heinz 57 Sauce
¼ cup honey

Cut the bell pepper into chunks and blanch in boiling water in a saucepan for 1 minute; drain. Cut each chicken breast into 4 pieces. Thread the chicken, bell pepper and pineapple alternately onto skewers. Combine the Heinz 57 Sauce and honey in a small bowl and mix well. Brush on the kabobs. Broil 6 inches from the heat source for 12 to 14 minutes or until the chicken is cooked through, turning and brushing with the steak sauce mixture 1 time.

GRILLED
VEGETABLE KABOBS

MAKES 4 SERVINGS

1 medium zucchini

1 medium eggplant

1 green bell pepper

1 small fresh pineapple, peeled and cored

2 small red onions, cut into quarters

8 cherry tomatoes

1 package
**EZ Marinader™ Classico®
Garlic and Herb Flavor**

Cut the zucchini, eggplant, bell pepper and pineapple into 1-inch pieces. Combine with the onions and cherry tomatoes in the bag of EZ Marinader Classico Garlic and Herb Flavor and seal the bag. Marinate in the refrigerator for 30 minutes, turning the bag occasionally to marinate evenly. Drain the vegetables and pineapple, reserving the marinade. Thread the vegetables and pineapple alternately onto 8 skewers. Grill over medium heat for 10 to 15 minutes or to desired degree of doneness, turning frequently and basting with the reserved marinade if desired. Serve over rice or couscous.

DRY-COOKED
GREEN BEANS

MAKES 4 SERVINGS

¼ cup vegetable oil

2 teaspoons minced gingerroot

1 teaspoon minced garlic

1 tablespoon soaked
and mashed black beans

1 pound short green beans

½ teaspoon salt

¼ teaspoon pepper

1 teaspoon sugar

2 tablespoons
Heinz Tomato Ketchup

¼ cup vegetable broth

¼ cup water

Heat the oil in a wok and add the gingerroot, garlic and black beans. Stir-fry for 3 minutes. Add the green beans and sprinkle with the salt and pepper. Stir-fry for 4 minutes. Add the sugar, Heinz Tomato Ketchup, vegetable broth and water and cook for 5 minutes or until the green beans are tender and the liquid has evaporated; the beans will appear wrinkled. Stir-fry the beans for 1 minute longer at this point.

PRE-GAME WARM-UPS

GAME DAY is a great way to gather friends and family for some quality time. To make sure your crowd has the energy they need to cheer the team on, stock your training table with a selection from these pre-game warm-ups.

APPLE PANCAKES
WITH CIDER SAUCE

MAKES 18 (4") PANCAKES & 2½ CUPS SAUCE

From Jerame Tuman

"This is my all-time favorite breakfast. My wife, Molly, often fixes this for me the morning after a game."

JERAME TUMAN

PANCAKES

2 medium apples
2 cups pancake/baking mix
1⅓ cups milk
1 egg
½ teaspoon cinnamon

CIDER SAUCE

1 cup sugar
2 tablespoons cornstarch
¼ teaspoon cinnamon
¼ teaspoon nutmeg
2 cups apple cider
2 tablespoons lemon juice
¼ cup (½ stick) butter
or margarine

FOR THE PANCAKES, grate the apples using a food grinder, if available. The grated apples should measure ¾ cup. Combine the baking mix, milk, egg and cinnamon in a bowl and beat with a rotary beater until smooth. Stir the apples into the batter.

Pour ¼ cup of the batter at a time onto a hot lightly greased griddle. Bake until bubbles appear on the surface and the underside is golden brown; turn. Bake until the remaining side is golden brown.

FOR THE SAUCE, combine the sugar, cornstarch, cinnamon and nutmeg in a saucepan and mix well. Stir in the apple cider and lemon juice. Cook until the mixture comes to a boil and thickens, stirring constantly. Boil for 1 minute, stirring constantly. Remove from the heat. Stir in the butter. Cover to keep warm. Serve warm with the pancakes.

Hint: Prepare the Cider Sauce after mixing the pancake batter but before baking so everything will be served warm.

PUMPKIN BREAD

MAKES 2 (5x9") LOAVES OR 3 (4x8") LOAVES   *From Shawn and Tim Lewis*

3⅓ cups flour

2 teaspoons baking soda

1½ teaspoons salt

1 teaspoon cinnamon

1 teaspoon ground cloves

½ teaspoon baking powder

2⅔ cups sugar

⅔ cup shortening

1 (16-ounce) can pumpkin

⅔ cup water

4 eggs

⅔ cup coarsely chopped nuts

⅔ cup raisins

Grease only the bottoms of the loaf pans. Mix the flour, baking soda, salt, cinnamon, cloves and baking powder in a bowl. Beat the sugar and shortening in a mixing bowl until light and fluffy, scraping the bowl occasionally. Add the pumpkin, water and eggs and beat until blended. Beat in the flour mixture. Stir in the nuts and raisins.

Spoon the batter into the prepared loaf pans. Bake at 350°F for 1 hour and 10 minutes or until a wooden pick inserted in the center of the loaves comes out clean. Cool in the pans for 10 minutes. Run a sharp knife around the sides of the loaves. Remove to a wire rack to cool completely. Slice as desired. Store, wrapped in foil or plastic wrap, in the refrigerator for up to 10 days.

"A wonderful Louisiana dish that pleases me to no end."

TIM LEWIS

BANANA BREAD

MAKES 1 LOAF OR 1 BUNDT CAKE

From Aaron Smith

"This is a great snack. Jaimie often fixes this for me for Saturday nights when we are in the hotel before the game."

AARON SMITH

2 cups flour
1 teaspoon baking soda
1 teaspoon salt
½ cup vegetable oil
½ cup packed brown sugar
½ cup sugar
2 eggs
3 ripe bananas, mashed
3 tablespoons milk
Sugar and cinnamon to taste

Mix the flour, baking soda and salt in a bowl. Combine the oil, brown sugar, sugar and eggs in a bowl and mix well. Stir in the flour mixture. Add the bananas and milk and mix well.

Spoon the batter into a greased loaf pan or bundt pan. Sprinkle sugar and cinnamon over the top. Bake at 350°F for 40 to 60 minutes or until the loaf or cake tests done. Cool in the pan for 10 minutes. Remove to a wire rack to cool completely. Slice as desired.

PUMPKIN CHOCOLATE CHIP MUFFINS

MAKES 1 DOZEN MUFFINS

From Jeff Hartings

1⅔ cups flour
1 cup sugar
1 tablespoon pumpkin pie spice
1 teaspoon baking soda
¼ teaspoon baking powder
¼ teaspoon salt
2 eggs
1 cup pumpkin
½ cup (1 stick) butter, melted
1 cup (6 ounces) chocolate chips
½ cup slivered almonds

Mix the flour, sugar, pumpkin pie spice, baking soda, baking powder and salt in a bowl. Whisk the eggs in a bowl until blended. Stir in the pumpkin and butter. Add the flour mixture to the pumpkin mixture and stir just until moistened. Fold in the chocolate chips and almonds.

Spoon the batter evenly into 12 muffin cups. Bake at 350°F for 20 to 25 minutes or until the muffins test done.

HEINZ FIELD

"A perfect seasonal treat to have around the house in the fall at Thanksgiving time."

JEFF HARTINGS

Queso Dip

48 ounces cream cheese, softened

3 cups Restaurant-Style Salsa

2 cups (¼-inch pieces) green onions

2 (14-ounce) cans black beans

1 (16-ounce) package frozen corn

1 (14-ounce) can jalapeño chiles

½ cup chopped fresh cilantro

Salt to taste

Beat the cream cheese in a 5-quart mixer bowl fitted with a paddle attachment for 1 to 5 minutes or until blended, scraping the bowl occasionally. Add the salsa, green onions, undrained beans, corn, jalapeño chiles, cilantro and salt to the cream cheese. Beat for 1 minute.

Spoon the cream cheese mixture into a microwave-safe ovenproof dish. Microwave on Medium for 8 minutes. Bake at 350°F for 15 minutes. Serve warm with tortilla chips.

Restaurant-Style
Salsa

MAKES 3 QUARTS

1 (6-pound 6-ounce) can
salsa-style diced tomatoes

4 cups (¼-inch pieces)
red onions

1 cup chopped fresh cilantro

1 (8-ounce) can chopped
jalapeño chiles

¼ cup lime juice

2 tablespoons olive oil

1 tablespoon cumin

Salt to taste

Combine the undrained tomatoes, onions, cilantro, jalapeño chiles, lime juice, olive oil, cumin and salt in a 5-quart container and mix well.

Chill, covered, for 2 to 3 hours before serving. Serve with tortilla chips.

GUACAMOLE

MAKES 2 CUPS

1 garlic clove

⅛ teaspoon salt

2 ounces red onion,
finely chopped

2 plum tomatoes,
seeded and chopped

¼ cup fresh lime juice

¼ cup fresh orange juice

1 serrano chile, seeded
and finely chopped

1 tablespoon minced
fresh cilantro

1 teaspoon kosher salt

½ teaspoon cracked pepper

6 avocados

Crush the garlic on a hard surface with the flat side of a knife. Sprinkle the garlic with ⅛ teaspoon salt and finely mince. The salt helps to work the garlic into a fine mince while chopping. Combine the garlic, onion, tomatoes, lime juice, orange juice, serrano chile, cilantro, 1 teaspoon kosher salt and pepper in a stainless steel bowl.

Peel the avocados and cut into halves. Remove the stones with the blade of a knife. Add the avocados to the tomato mixture and coarsely mash the avocado with a fork while combining the ingredients; be sure to leave a few chunks of avocado. Chill, covered, for 2 hours or longer to allow the flavors to blend. Serve with tortilla chips.

SOUTHWEST CAVIAR

MAKES 6 CUPS

3 (16-ounce) cans
black-eyed peas, drained

1 tablespoon Heinz
Gourmet Wine Vinegar

½ cup Heinz 57 Sauce

1 cup chopped onion

1 medium tomato,
seeded and chopped

½ cup chopped
green bell pepper

½ cup chopped
red bell pepper

1 jalapeño chile,
seeded and chopped

1 tablespoon chopped
fresh cilantro

1 garlic clove, minced

½ teaspoon chili powder

¼ teaspoon salt

¼ teaspoon cumin

Combine 1½ cups of the black-eyed peas, the
Heinz Gourmet Wine Vinegar and Heinz 57 Sauce
in a food processor or blender. Process until smooth.
Combine the pureed black-eyed pea mixture,
remaining black-eyed peas, onion, tomato, bell
peppers, jalapeño chile, cilantro, garlic, chili powder,
salt and cumin in a bowl and mix well. Chill, covered,
until serving time. Serve as a dip with corn chips or
over lettuce as a salad.

PLAYBOOK

Assuming a person
uses one tablespoon
of Heinz Ketchup
on a hot dog,
each bottle on the
Heinz Field
Jumbotron would
provide enough of the
red stuff to top
3.2 million hot dogs –
that's about
ten hot dogs
for each resident
within the
city of Pittsburgh.

THE SON-IN-LAW DIP

MAKES 4 SERVINGS   *From Alan Faneca*

Chopped jalapeño chiles to taste
**8 ounces cream cheese or
low-fat cream cheese**
1 can Hormel® Chili with Beans
Shredded Cheddar cheese

Drain the jalapeño chiles, reserving the liquid. Heat the cream cheese in a 6x6-inch baking dish in a 350°F oven until soft. Remove from the oven. Spread the cream cheese evenly in the dish and top with the chili.

For a spicy dip, pour the reserved jalapeño liquid over the prepared layers. Sprinkle with cheese and the jalapeño chiles. Bake at 350°F for 30 minutes. Serve warm with tortilla chips.

BEEF DIP

MAKES 8 HORS D'OEUVRE SERVINGS

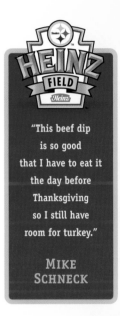 *From Mike Schneck*

2½ ounces dried beef

8 ounces cream cheese, softened

½ cup sour cream

2 tablespoons milk

½ teaspoon garlic salt

¼ teaspoon pepper

¼ cup chopped green bell pepper

2 tablespoons minced green onions

Rinse the dried beef and blot dry; shred. Combine the cream cheese, sour cream, milk, garlic, salt and pepper in a bowl and mix well. Stir in the dried beef, bell pepper and green onions.

Spoon the dried beef mixture into an 8- or 9-inch round baking dish. Bake at 350°F for 20 minutes or until brown and bubbly. Serve warm with assorted party crackers.

> "This beef dip is so good that I have to eat it the day before Thanksgiving so I still have room for turkey."
>
> MIKE SCHNECK

Santa Fe
Potato Pancakes

MAKES 6 SERVINGS

PLAYBOOK

Approximately
4,500 footballs
could fit into each
Heinz Ketchup bottle
on the Heinz Field
Jumbotron scoreboard.

1 (26-ounce) package
Ore-Ida® Country Style
Hash Browns
1 cup (4 ounces) shredded
Pepper Jack cheese
½ cup milk
½ cup sour cream
¼ cup sliced green onions
3 tablespoons vegetable oil
½ teaspoon salt
½ teaspoon cumin
½ teaspoon pepper
¼ cup flour
Vegetable oil

Combine the Ore-Ida Country Style Hash Browns, cheese, milk, sour cream, green onions, 3 tablespoons oil, salt, cumin and pepper in a bowl and mix well. Let stand for 10 minutes. Stir in the flour.

Drop the potato mixture by ¼ cupfuls into hot oil in a large skillet. Fry over medium-high heat for 6 minutes or until golden brown on both sides, turning once. Drain on paper towels. Serve topped with additional sour cream and chopped fresh cilantro if desired.

POTTED
CHEESE SPREAD

MAKES 1¾ CUPS

4 cups (16 ounces) shredded Cheddar cheese

8 ounces cream cheese, softened

¼ cup Heinz Chili Sauce

2 tablespoons dry sherry

½ teaspoon dry mustard

Combine the Cheddar cheese, Heinz Chili Sauce, sherry and dry mustard in a bowl and mix well. Spoon the cheese mixture into a crock or serving dish. Chill, covered, for several hours. Serve with assorted party crackers and/or apple slices. You may store the spread, covered, in the refrigerator for up to 1 week.

ZESTY
WALNUT SPREAD

MAKES 1½ CUPS

8 ounces cream cheese, softened

¼ cup Heinz Tomato Ketchup

½ teaspoon lemon juice

½ to ¼ teaspoon hot pepper sauce

½ cup coarsely chopped walnuts, toasted

Beat the cream cheese, Heinz Tomato Ketchup, lemon juice and hot pepper sauce in a mixing bowl until blended, scraping the bowl occasionally. Stir in the walnuts. Chill, covered, until serving time. Serve with assorted party crackers and/or vegetable dippers.

MINESTRONE WITH
PESTO MEATBALLS

MAKES 6 SERVINGS

MEATBALLS

8 ounces ground beef

⅓ cup Classico® Traditional Basil Pesto Sauce & Spread

¼ cup dry bread crumbs

1 egg, lightly beaten

MINESTRONE

3 cups water

1 (26-ounce) jar Classico® di Napoli Tomato & Basil Pasta Sauce

1 (16-ounce) can garbanzo beans, drained

1 small zucchini, sliced

1 small summer squash, sliced

1 tablespoon Wyler's® Beef Flavor Instant Bouillon Granules

1 cup elbow macaroni, cooked and drained

FOR THE MEATBALLS, combine the ground beef, 3 tablespoons of the Classico Traditional Basil Pesto Sauce & Spread, bread crumbs and egg in a bowl and mix well. Shape the ground beef mixture into 1-inch meatballs. Arrange the meatballs in a single layer in a shallow baking pan. Bake at 350°F for 20 minutes or until cooked through; drain.

FOR THE SOUP, combine the water, Classico di Napoli Tomato & Basil Pasta Sauce, beans, zucchini, summer squash and Wyler's Beef Flavor Bouillon Granules in a stockpot. Bring to a boil, stirring occasionally; reduce the heat.

Simmer, covered, for 15 minutes, stirring occasionally. Stir in the meatballs and pasta. Simmer just until heated through. Ladle into soup bowls. Serve with the remaining pesto sauce and spread.

ROASTED
TOMATO BISQUE

MAKES 8 SERVINGS

3 pounds Roma tomatoes,
cored and cut into ½-inch slices

¼ cup olive oil

2 tablespoons chopped shallots

1 tablespoon minced fresh thyme

1 tablespoon chopped fresh basil

1 tablespoon minced
sun-dried tomatoes

1 tablespoon chopped
fresh parsley

1 teaspoon chopped garlic

1 teaspoon freshly ground pepper

Salt to taste

2 cups half-and-half

1 (26-ounce) jar Classico®
di Capri Sun-Dried Tomato
Alfredo Pasta Sauce

Toss the sliced tomatoes, olive oil, shallots, thyme, basil, sun-dried tomatoes, parsley, garlic, pepper and salt in a bowl until coated. Arrange the tomato slices in a single layer on a baking sheet lined with baking parchment.

Roast at 450°F for 20 to 25 minutes or until light brown. Place the roasted tomatoes with pan drippings and the half-and-half in a food processor or blender. Process until pureed. Pour the tomato puree into a saucepan and stir in the Classico Sun-Dried Tomato Alfredo Sauce. Bring to a simmer, stirring occasionally. Simmer for 10 minutes, stirring occasionally. Ladle into soup bowls.

SOUP DI NAPOLI

MAKES 6 SERVINGS

8 ounces small shell pasta

8 ounces Italian sausage links, sliced

1 small zucchini, sliced (about 1 cup)

1 small summer squash, sliced (about 1 cup)

½ cup chopped onion

3 cups water

1 (26-ounce) jar Classico® di Napoli Tomato & Basil Pasta Sauce

1 (16-ounce) can garbanzo beans, drained

1 tablespoon Wyler's® Beef Flavor Instant Bouillon Granules

Cook the pasta using the package directions; drain. Brown the sausage in a large saucepan, stirring frequently. Add the zucchini, summer squash and onion and mix well. Cook until the vegetables are tender, stirring frequently. Stir in the water, Classico di Napoli Tomato & Basil Pasta Sauce, beans and Wyler's Beef Flavor Instant Bouillon Granules.

Bring to a boil; reduce the heat. Simmer, covered, for 15 minutes, stirring occasionally. Stir in the pasta. Simmer just until heated through. Ladle into soup bowls.

MUSSELS
MARINARA

MAKES 10 SERVINGS

PLAYBOOK

The H.J. Heinz
Company is no stranger
to innovative signage.
Heinz designed
New York City's
first large outdoor
electric sign in 1900,
a six-story-high sign
that promoted
Heinz pickles and
other products
and touted the
company's famous
phrase, "57 Varieties."

¼ cup olive oil

½ cup chopped garlic

3 pounds green-lipped mussels,
scrubbed and debearded

1 cup white wine

2 cups Classico®
di Campania Sweet Basil
Marinara Pasta Sauce

¼ cup chopped fresh parsley

Heat the olive oil in a heavy sauté pan over medium-high heat. Sauté the garlic in the hot oil for 30 seconds; do not burn. Stir in the mussels and wine. Steam, covered, for 5 minutes or until the mussels open.

Add the Classico di Campania Sweet Basil Marinara Pasta Sauce and parsley to the mussel mixture and mix well. Cook for 2 minutes, stirring occasionally. Serve with Italian bread.

BAKED PASTA RAGU

MAKES 16 SERVINGS

TOMATO SAUCE

½ cup olive oil

8 ounces onions,
cut into ¼-inch pieces

2 ounces garlic, chopped

½ cup red wine

1 (6-pound 6-ounce) can
diced tomatoes in juice

2 ounces fresh basil, chopped

1 ounce fresh oregano, chopped

Salt and pepper to taste

PASTA AND ASSEMBLY

2 pounds penne or rigatoni

8 ounces (2 cups) mozzarella
cheese, shredded

FOR THE SAUCE, heat the olive oil in a large heavy stockpot. Cook the onions in the hot oil over medium-high heat for 12 to 15 minutes or until golden brown and caramelized, stirring frequently. Stir in the garlic. Cook for 5 minutes, stirring frequently. Add the wine gradually, stirring constantly.

Cook for 5 minutes, stirring frequently. Stir in the undrained diced tomatoes. Simmer over low heat for 30 minutes, stirring frequently. Add the basil, oregano, salt and pepper and mix well. Remove from the heat. Let stand for 5 minutes. Cover to keep warm.

FOR THE PASTA, cook the pasta using the package directions; drain. Add the pasta to the warm sauce and mix well. Spoon the pasta mixture into a large baking dish and sprinkle with the cheese. Bake at 350°F for 10 minutes.

RAP WRAPS

MAKES 10 SERVINGS

**2 or 3 slices American
or Cheddar cheese**
1 pound frankfurters
Heinz Tomato Ketchup
**1 (12-ounce) package
refrigerator biscuits**

Cut the cheese into thin slices. Cut a slit lengthwise
in each frankfurter to within ½ inch of the ends.
Place 2 or 3 slices of cheese in each slit. Pour
Heinz Tomato Ketchup over the top of each prepared
frankfurter. Roll each biscuit into a 4-inch circle.
Wrap a biscuit around each prepared frankfurter.
Arrange cheese side up on an ungreased baking sheet.
Bake at 400°F for 8 to 12 minutes or until golden
brown. Serve with additional ketchup.

BUFFALO
CHICKEN WINGS

MAKES 4 SERVINGS

CHICKEN WINGS

24 chicken wings

5 tablespoons butter

3 tablespoons hot sauce

Jack Daniel's® Original
No.7 Barbecue Recipe™
Grilling Sauce

BLUE CHEESE SAUCE

1 cup yogurt

1 tablespoon Heinz
Red Wine Vinegar

Juice of ½ lemon

1 garlic clove, minced

1 teaspoon sugar

⅛ teaspoon Heinz
Worcestershire Sauce

Salt and pepper to taste

¾ cup crumbled blue cheese

Celery sticks

FOR THE WINGS, cut the wings into halves at the joint, discarding the tips. Place the wings in a bowl. Heat the butter in a saucepan until melted. Stir in the hot sauce and mix well. Pour the butter mixture over the wings, turning to coat. Let stand at room temperature for 30 minutes, stirring occasionally.

Arrange the wings on a grill rack. Grill over medium-hot coals until the wings are golden brown and cooked through, turning and basting occasionally with Jack Daniel's Original No.7 Barbecue Recipe Grilling Sauce.

FOR THE SAUCE, combine the yogurt, Heinz Red Wine Vinegar, lemon juice, garlic, sugar, Heinz Worcestershire Sauce, salt and pepper in a bowl and mix well. Fold in the blue cheese; the sauce should have a lumpy consistency. Serve the wings with the sauce and celery sticks.

TRICOLOR TORTELLINI
WITH SPINACH & TOMATO IN ALFREDO SAUCE

MAKES 5 TO 6 SERVINGS

PLAYBOOK

If both Heinz Ketchup
bottles on the
Heinz Field Jumbotron
were emptied,
the entire football
field would be
covered with ¾ of an
inch of ketchup.

10 ounces tricolor tortellini

2 tablespoons olive oil

3 ounces plum tomatoes,
seeded and chopped

2 ounces (1½ cups) fresh
spinach, stems removed

¼ teaspoon minced garlic

5 ounces Classico®
di Roma Alfredo Sauce

1 ounce (¼ cup)
Parmesan cheese, grated

¼ teaspoon chopped fresh basil

¼ teaspoon chopped fresh
flat-leaf parsley

Cook the pasta using the package directions; drain. Heat the olive oil in a sauté pan. Sauté the tomatoes, spinach and garlic in the hot oil. Add the pasta to the tomato mixture and mix well. Stir in the Classico di Roma Alfredo Sauce.

Bring to a boil, stirring occasionally. Remove from the heat. Sprinkle with the cheese, basil and parsley. Serve immediately.

SHEPHERD'S PIE

MAKES 4 TO 6 SERVINGS

1 pound lean ground beef

1 medium onion, chopped

1 tablespoon vegetable oil

1 (16-ounce) package
frozen mixed vegetables

½ cup Heinz Tomato Ketchup

¼ cup tomato juice

1 tablespoon
Heinz Yellow Mustard

1 teaspoon Heinz
Worcestershire Sauce

1 teaspoon salt

1 teaspoon pepper

4 servings prepared
mashed potatoes

Brown the ground beef and onion in the oil in a large skillet, stirring until the ground beef is crumbly; drain. Stir in the mixed vegetables, Heinz Tomato Ketchup, tomato juice, Heinz Yellow Mustard, Heinz Worcestershire Sauce, salt and pepper. Bring to a boil; reduce the heat.

Simmer for 15 minutes, stirring occasionally. Spoon the ground beef mixture into a 2-quart baking dish. Spread the mashed potatoes over the top. Bake at 350°F for 15 to 20 minutes or until the potatoes are light brown.

HALFTIME HIGHLIGHTS

SCORE POINTS, even when our team is in the locker room, with these hearty halftime dishes. They're perfect for your party line-up. The only requests for instant replays you'll be getting will be for second helpings.

TURKEY CHILI
WITH WHITE BEANS

MAKES 8 SERVINGS

1 tablespoon vegetable oil

2 onions, chopped

1 teaspoon oregano

1½ teaspoons cumin

1½ pounds lean ground turkey

¼ cup chili powder

2 bay leaves

1 tablespoon unsweetened
cocoa powder

1½ teaspoons salt

¼ teaspoon ground cinnamon

1 (28-ounce) can whole tomatoes

3 cups beef stock

1 (8-ounce) can tomato sauce

3 (15-ounce) cans
small white beans

Heat the oil in a heavy large stockpot over medium heat. Add the onions. Sauté until golden brown. Add the oregano and cumin. Cook for 1 minute, stirring constantly. Increase the heat to medium-high. Add the turkey and brown, stirring until crumbly. Stir in the chili powder, bay leaves, cocoa powder, salt and cinnamon. Add the tomatoes, breaking up with the back of a spoon. Stir in the stock and tomato sauce. Bring to a boil. Reduce the heat. Simmer for 45 minutes, stirring occasionally.

Add the beans and stir to combine. Cook for 10 minutes. Remove and discard the bay leaves.

Ladle into soup bowls. Garnish with red onion, cilantro, and yogurt or light sour cream.

PASTA DI GENOA WITH
TURKEY MEATBALLS

MAKES 4 SERVINGS

8 ounces mostaccioli rigate pasta

12 ounces ground turkey

½ cup dry Italian seasoned bread crumbs

¼ cup (1 ounce) grated Parmesan cheese

1 egg, beaten

2 teaspoons Wyler's® Chicken Flavor Instant Bouillon Granules

1 (26-ounce) jar Classico® di Genoa Spicy Tomato & Pesto Pasta Sauce

Cook the pasta using the package directions; drain. Set aside and keep warm.

Combine the turkey, bread crumbs, Parmesan cheese, egg and Wyler's Chicken Flavor Instant Bouillon Granules and mix well. Shape into 1-inch meatballs. Place in a large saucepan. Pour the Classico di Genoa Spicy Tomato & Pesto Pasta Sauce over the meatballs. Bring to a boil. Reduce the heat. Simmer, covered, for 20 minutes or until the meatballs are cooked through, stirring occasionally. Serve with the hot pasta.

HEARTY
MEAT LASAGNA

MAKES 8 SERVINGS

● *From John Fiala*

"My wife, Meg, fixes this as a great, hearty meal when I need carbohydrates before a game. There is always enough left for other meals."

JOHN FIALA

2 pounds ground beef
1 garlic clove, minced
1 tablespoon chopped parsley
1 tablespoon basil
½ teaspoon salt
1 (16-ounce) can tomatoes
2 (6-ounce) cans tomato paste
2 (12-ounce) containers ricotta cheese
2 eggs, beaten
1 teaspoon salt
½ teaspoon pepper
2 tablespoons chopped parsley
½ cup (2 ounces) grated Parmesan cheese
1 (10-ounce) package no-bake lasagna noodles
3 packages mozzarella cheese, sliced thin

Brown the ground beef in a skillet, stirring until crumbly; drain. Stir in the garlic, 1 tablespoon parsley, basil, salt, tomatoes and tomato paste. Bring to a simmer. Simmer for 45 to 60 minutes or until thick, stirring occasionally.

Combine the ricotta cheese, eggs, salt, pepper, 2 tablespoons parsley and Parmesan cheese in a bowl and mix well.

Layer the noodles, cheese mixture, meat mixture and mozzarella cheese slices ½ at a time in a 9 x 13-inch baking dish. Cover with foil. Bake at 350°F for 40 minutes. Remove the foil and bake for 30 to 40 minutes or until hot and bubbly.

CLASSIC
TWO-SAUCE LASAGNA

MAKES 10 TO 12 SERVINGS

1 pound bulk Italian sausage or ground beef

1 (15-ounce) container ricotta cheese

1 (10-ounce) package frozen chopped spinach, thawed and drained

2 cups (8 ounces) shredded mozzarella cheese

2 tablespoons grated Parmesan cheese

2 eggs

1 (26-ounce) jar Classico® di Campania Sweet Basil Marinara Pasta Sauce

12 no-bake lasagna noodles

1 (17-ounce) jar Classico® di Capri Sun-Dried Tomato Alfredo Pasta Sauce

2 tablespoons grated Parmesan cheese

Brown the sausage in a skillet, stirring until crumbly; drain. Combine the ricotta cheese, spinach, mozzarella cheese, 2 tablespoons Parmesan cheese and eggs in a bowl and mix well.

Spread 1 cup of the Classico di Campania Sweet Basil Marinara Pasta Sauce evenly over the bottom of a 9 x 13-inch baking dish. Layer 4 lasagna noodles, ½ of the cheese mixture, 1 cup marinara sauce and ½ of the cooked sausage over the marinara sauce. Continue layering with 4 lasagna noodles, the remaining cheese mixture, 1 cup marinara sauce, the remaining cooked sausage and the remaining 4 lasagna noodles. Spread the Classico di Capri Sun-Dried Tomato Alfredo Pasta Sauce evenly over the layers. Sprinkle with 2 tablespoons Parmesan cheese.

Bake, covered, at 350°F for 40 minutes. Remove the cover and bake for 15 minutes or until bubbly. Let stand for 10 minutes.

MEMA'S LASAGNA

MAKES 8 SERVINGS

From Traci and Mark Bruener

"You'll never leave the table hungry with this dish. Traci lured me in with her Mema's Lasagna."

MARK BRUENER

1 pound mild Italian sausage

1 pound ground beef

1½ teaspoons basil

1½ teaspoons minced garlic

2 teaspoons salt

2 (15-ounce) cans diced tomatoes

1 (12-ounce) can tomato paste

3 cups cottage cheese

½ cup (2 ounces) grated Parmesan cheese

2 tablespoons parsley flakes

2 eggs, beaten

1 teaspoon salt

1 package no-bake lasagna noodles

3 cups (12 ounces) shredded mozzarella cheese

Brown the sausage and ground beef in a skillet, stirring until crumbly; drain. Add the basil, garlic, salt, tomatoes and tomato paste and mix well. Bring to a simmer and simmer for 20 minutes.

Combine the cottage cheese, Parmesan cheese, parsley, eggs and salt in a bowl and mix well.

Layer the noodles, cottage cheese mixture, mozzarella cheese and meat sauce ½ at a time in a greased 9 x 13-inch baking dish. Bake at 375°F for 40 minutes.

Italian Style
Meat Loaf

MAKES 4 TO 6 SERVINGS

From Josh Miller

1 to 1½ pounds ground beef
2 eggs
Salt and freshly
ground pepper to taste
½ cup rice
⅓ cup grated Parmesan cheese
1 small onion, chopped
¼ cup chopped fresh parsley
¾ cup bread crumbs
1 (8-ounce) can tomato sauce
1 (16-ounce) can tomato sauce
2 cups water
5 or 6 red-skinned potatoes

Combine the ground beef, eggs, salt, pepper, rice, Parmesan cheese, onion, parsley, bread crumbs and 8-ounce can of tomato sauce in a bowl and mix well. Shape into a loaf. Place in a baking dish. Pour the 16-ounce can of tomato sauce over the meat loaf. Pour the water into the pan. Cut the potatoes into halves and place along the sides of the meat loaf. Bake at 350°F for 1½ hours.

"Angie's Meat Loaf
is magical!
I can smell it from
the driveway.
It's like a great
old 70's song,
it always puts me
in a good mood!"

JOSH
MILLER

EGGPLANT
PARMIGIANA

2 large eggplant, cut into
½-inch-thick rounds

Salt

Flour

Olive oil for frying

1 (26-ounce) jar
Classico® di Parma
Four Cheese Pasta Sauce

1½ cups (6 ounces)
shredded mozzarella cheese

⅓ cup freshly grated
Parmesan cheese

Sprinkle the eggplant rounds lightly with salt.
Let stand for 60 to 90 minutes; pat dry. Dredge in
the flour, shaking off the excess.

Heat 6 tablespoons of the olive oil in a large skillet
over medium heat. Add 2 or 3 eggplant slices and
cook until golden brown on both sides, adding
additional olive oil as needed. Place on paper towels
to drain. Repeat with the remaining eggplant slices.

Spread a thin layer of Classico di Parma Four Cheese
Pasta Sauce evenly over the bottom of a 7 x 11-inch
baking dish. Layer ⅓ of the eggplant, ⅓ of the
remaining pasta sauce, ½ of the mozzarella cheese
and ⅓ of the Parmesan cheese over the sauce.
Continue layering with ½ of the remaining eggplant,
½ of the remaining pasta sauce, the remaining
mozzarella cheese and ½ of the remaining Parmesan
cheese. Continue layering with the remaining
eggplant, remaining pasta sauce and remaining
Parmesan cheese.

Bake at 350°F for 25 to 30 minutes. Let stand for
15 minutes. Serve with additional Parmesan cheese
if desired.

Tuna and Eggplant
Parmigiana

1 (9-ounce) can solid white albacore tuna, drained

⅓ cup chopped onion

2 garlic cloves, minced

1 tablespoon olive oil or vegetable oil

2 large tomatoes, chopped

1 cup Classico® di Napoli Tomato & Basil Pasta Sauce

⅓ cup tomato paste

2 teaspoons dried Italian seasoning, crushed

¼ teaspoon pepper

1 eggplant, peeled

⅔ cup grated Parmesan or Romano cheese

1 cup (4 ounces) shredded low-fat mozzarella cheese

3 tablespoons minced parsley

Break the tuna into chunks. Sauté the onion and garlic in the olive oil in a skillet for 3 minutes or until tender. Stir in the tomatoes, Classico di Napoli Tomato & Basil Pasta Sauce, tomato paste, Italian seasoning and pepper. Bring to a boil. Reduce the heat. Simmer for 10 minutes, stirring occasionally. Stir the tuna into the sauce. Remove from the heat and set aside.

Cut the eggplant crosswise into ¼-inch-thick slices. Bring enough water to cover the eggplant to a boil in a large saucepan. Add the eggplant. Simmer for 20 minutes or until tender. Drain and pat dry with paper towels.

Combine the Parmesan cheese and mozzarella cheese in a bowl and mix well.

Layer the eggplant, tomato sauce and cheeses ⅓ at a time in an 8 x 12-inch baking dish. Sprinkle the parsley over the top. Bake at 350°F for 25 to 30 minutes or until hot and bubbly.

CHICKEN CACCIATORE

MAKES 4 SERVINGS

2 tablespoons flour

1 teaspoon Italian seasoning

4 boneless skinless chicken breasts (about 1 pound)

2 tablespoons olive oil

2 cups sliced fresh mushrooms

½ cup chopped onion

1 (26-ounce) jar Classico® di Sorrento Roasted Garlic Pasta Sauce

1 cup (4 ounces) shredded mozzarella or provolone cheese

8 ounces fettuccine, cooked

Combine the flour and Italian seasoning in a shallow dish and mix well. Dredge the chicken in the flour mixture, shaking off the excess. Heat the olive oil in a large skillet over medium-high heat. Add the chicken and cook until brown. Remove the chicken from the skillet. Add the mushrooms and onion to the skillet. Cook until tender, stirring constantly. Add the Classico di Sorrento Roasted Garlic Pasta Sauce and chicken. Simmer, covered, for 15 minutes or until the chicken is cooked through. Sprinkle the cheese over the chicken. Serve with the hot fettuccine.

CHICKEN
MONTEREY

MAKES 4 SERVINGS

1 (12-ounce) can black beans
1 pound boneless skinless chicken breasts
1 tablespoon vegetable oil
½ teaspoon chili powder
1 (12-ounce) can whole kernel corn, drained
½ cup Heinz Tomato Ketchup
1 large tomato, chopped

Drain the beans, reserving ½ cup of the liquid. Brown the chicken in hot oil in a large skillet. Sprinkle with the chili powder. Add the corn, Heinz Tomato Ketchup, beans and reserved liquid. Simmer, covered, for 5 to 7 minutes, stirring occasionally. Divide evenly among four plates. Top with the chopped tomato.

CHICKEN SKILLET

MAKES 4 SERVINGS

4 boneless skinless
chicken breasts

1 (14-ounce) can
stewed tomatoes

1½ cups chicken broth

1 cup rice

½ cup Heinz Tomato Ketchup

½ cup chopped green
bell pepper

½ teaspoon salt

Brown the chicken on both sides in a large nonstick skillet sprayed with nonstick cooking spray. Remove the chicken and set aside.

Combine the stewed tomatoes, broth, rice, Heinz Tomato Ketchup, bell pepper and salt in the skillet and stir to combine. Bring to a simmer. Simmer, covered, for 1 minute. Add the chicken. Cook, covered, for 10 to 15 minutes or until the chicken is cooked through and the rice is tender, stirring once.

STUFFED
TOMATOES

⅔ pound ground beef or pork

1 onion, chopped

1 tablespoon rice wine
or dry sherry

1 teaspoon salt

1 tablespoon soy sauce

1 egg white

¼ teaspoon pepper

2 tablespoons
Heinz Tomato Ketchup

2 tablespoons cornstarch

8 firm tomatoes

8 cups boiling water

1 teaspoon cornstarch

7 tablespoons vegetable oil

1 tablespoon sugar

2 tablespoons soy sauce

2 tablespoons beef broth
or chicken broth

½ cup water

4 cups water

2 teaspoons cornstarch

2 teaspoons water

Combine the ground beef or pork, onion, rice wine, salt, 1 tablespoon soy sauce, egg white, pepper, Heinz Tomato Ketchup and 2 tablespoons cornstarch in a bowl and mix well.

Cut the skin of each tomato from top to bottom. Submerge 1 tomato in the boiling water for 10 seconds. Remove the skin and cut the tomato in half. Remove and discard the seeds and pulp. Repeat with the remaining tomatoes. Sprinkle 1 teaspoon cornstarch over the insides of the tomato shells. Fill each shell with the ground beef mixture.

Heat the oil in a large skillet. Place the filled tomato shells filled side down in the skillet. Cook for 3 minutes or until brown. Remove and place filled side down in a baking dish. Combine the sugar, 2 tablespoons soy sauce, beef broth and ½ cup water in a small bowl and mix well. Pour over the tomatoes. Cover the baking dish.

Bring 4 cups water to a boil in a large stockpot over high heat. Place the baking dish on a steamer rack over the boiling water. Steam for 20 minutes or until the ground beef mixture is cooked through. Place the tomatoes filled side up on a serving plate.

Pour the liquid in the baking dish into a small saucepan. Dissolve 2 teaspoons cornstarch in 2 teaspoons water in a small bowl. Add to the liquid. Cook until thickened, stirring constantly. Pour over the tomatoes.

Southwestern
Corn Medley

MAKES 4 SERVINGS

1 small zucchini

3 cups frozen whole kernel corn

1 tomato, chopped

½ cup **Heinz Tomato Ketchup**

1 teaspoon chili powder

⅛ teaspoon cumin

¼ cup sliced green onions

1 tablespoon
chopped fresh cilantro

½ teaspoon lime juice

Cut the zucchini into halves lengthwise. Cut each half into ¼-inch slices. Combine the zucchini, corn, tomato, Heinz Tomato Ketchup, chili powder and cumin in a medium saucepan. Cook for 10 to 12 minutes or until the vegetables are tender, stirring occasionally. Stir in the green onions, cilantro and lime juice.

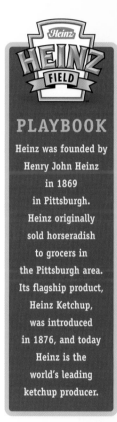

PLAYBOOK

Heinz was founded by
Henry John Heinz
in 1869
in Pittsburgh.
Heinz originally
sold horseradish
to grocers in
the Pittsburgh area.
Its flagship product,
Heinz Ketchup,
was introduced
in 1876, and today
Heinz is the
world's leading
ketchup producer.

SAUSAGE
SPINACH PIE

MAKES TWO 9-INCH PIES

From Matt Cushing

"One of my favorites. Spinach Pie is a very filling dinner that hits the spot after long workouts. Makes enough for two meals when it's just Angie and me eating."

MATT CUSHING

4 refrigerator pie pastries

1 pound cooked sweet or hot Italian sausage, chopped

2 (10-ounce) packages frozen chopped spinach, thawed and drained

5 eggs plus 1 egg white, reserve the yolk for glaze

16 ounces (4 cups) mozzarella cheese, shredded

1 teaspoon salt

1 (15-ounce) container ricotta cheese

1 teaspoon chopped garlic

Freshly ground pepper to taste

1 egg yolk, beaten

Line 2 pie plates with a pie pastry.

Combine the sausage, spinach, eggs, egg white, mozzarella cheese, salt, ricotta cheese, garlic and pepper in a bowl and mix well. Pour half into each of the prepared pie plates. Pat the filling down to level the surface. Top each pie with 1 of the remaining pastries, sealing the edges and cutting vents. Brush the tops with the beaten egg yolk to glaze.

Bake at 375°F for 1¼ hours. Let stand for 5 to 10 minutes.

PASTA AND CHICKEN
DI TOSCANA

MAKES 4 SERVINGS

12 ounces bow tie pasta

8 ounces boneless skinless chicken breasts

½ cup dry white wine or water

1 teaspoon Italian seasoning

1 (26-ounce) jar Classico® di Toscana Portobello Mushroom Pasta Sauce

½ cup frozen peas

Cook the pasta using the package directions; drain. Set aside and keep warm.

Combine the chicken and wine in a medium skillet. Sprinkle the chicken with the Italian seasoning. Bring to a simmer. Simmer, covered, for 20 minutes or until the chicken is cooked through. Remove the chicken and cut into slices. Return the chicken to the skillet. Add the Classico di Toscana Portobello Mushroom Pasta Sauce and peas. Cook until heated through. Serve with the bow tie pasta.

CHICKEN
WITH TOMATO SAUCE

MAKES 4 SERVINGS

12 ounces boneless skinless
chicken breasts

MARINADE
½ teaspoon salt
2 teaspoons rice wine
or dry sherry
1 teaspoon soy sauce
1 egg yolk
⅛ teaspoon pepper

TOMATO SAUCE
2 tablespoons sugar
¼ cup chicken broth
2 tablespoons water
½ teaspoon salt
2 teaspoons cornstarch
1 teaspoon sesame oil
¼ cup Heinz Tomato Ketchup

ASSEMBLY
6 tablespoons cornstarch
2 tablespoons flour
8 cups vegetable oil for
deep frying
1 tablespoon vegetable oil

Cut the chicken into very thin 1½ x 2-inch slices.
Place in a shallow dish.

FOR THE MARINADE, combine ½ teaspoon salt,
rice wine, soy sauce, egg yolk and pepper in a
small bowl and mix well. Pour over the chicken.

FOR THE SAUCE, combine the sugar, chicken broth,
water, ½ teaspoon salt, 2 teaspoons cornstarch,
sesame oil and Heinz Tomato Ketchup in a bowl
and mix well. Set aside.

TO ASSEMBLE, combine 6 tablespoons cornstarch
and flour in a shallow dish and mix well. Drain the
chicken, discarding the marinade. Dredge in the
cornstarch mixture, shaking to remove the excess.
Heat 8 cups oil in a wok to 350°F over medium heat.
Reduce the heat to low. Place the coated chicken
strips in the hot oil. Cook until golden brown and
cooked through. Remove from the oil, draining over
the wok. Arrange on a serving platter.

Remove and discard the oil in the wok, reserving
1 teaspoon. Heat the wok over medium heat.
Stir in the ketchup mixture. Bring to a boil. Cook
until the sauce thickens. Stir in 1 tablespoon oil.
Pour over the chicken. Garnish with tomato slices.
Serve immediately.

CARROTS
SAUCILY SPICED

MAKES 4 TO 6 SERVINGS

1 pound carrots, cut into
½-inch diagonal slices
Salt to taste
1½ tablespoons light brown sugar
1 tablespoon butter or margarine
⅛ teaspoon allspice
¼ cup Heinz Tomato Ketchup

Bring enough water to cover the carrots to a boil in a saucepan. Add a small amount of salt. Add the carrots. Cook until tender-crisp; drain.

Combine the brown sugar, butter, allspice and Heinz Tomato Ketchup in a medium skillet or saucepan. Cook until heated through, stirring frequently. Add the carrots. Cook until the carrots are glazed and heated through, turning frequently.

PLAYBOOK

In 1896, H.J. Heinz noticed an advertisement for "21 styles of shoes". He decided that his own products were not styles, but varieties. Although there were many more than 57 foods in production at the time, because he thought the number sounded mystical, Heinz adopted the slogan "57 Varieties."

CHICKEN NOODLE
CASSEROLE

MAKES 6 TO 8 SERVINGS

From Jennifer Maddox

"This is the first thing that I cooked for my wife, Jen, when we first met. This was my mother's old recipe, and now Jen can make it better than my mother or me."

TOMMY MADDOX

1 (8-ounce) package
wide egg noodles, cooked
4 boneless chicken breasts,
cooked and chopped
1 (10-ounce) can
cream of chicken soup
1 (10-ounce) can
cream of mushroom soup
½ cup milk
2 tablespoons sour cream
½ teaspoon garlic powder
½ teaspoon onion powder
Salt and pepper to taste
1 cup shredded Colby cheese

Combine the noodles, chicken, soups, milk, sour cream, garlic powder, onion powder, salt and pepper in a bowl and mix well. Spoon evenly into a 9 x 13-inch baking dish. Sprinkle the Colby cheese over the top. Bake at 400°F for 20 minutes or until the mixture is heated through and the cheese begins to brown. Let stand for 5 to 10 minutes.

LAYERED ANGEL HAIR
AND SAUSAGE BAKE

MAKES 4 SERVINGS

8 ounces angel hair pasta

1 egg, beaten

⅓ cup grated Parmesan cheese

1 tablespoon margarine or butter

2 cups (8 ounces)
shredded mozzarella cheese

1 (26-ounce) jar Classico®
di Abruzzi Italian Sausage with
Peppers & Onions Pasta Sauce

Cook the pasta using the package directions; drain. Combine the cooked pasta, egg, Parmesan cheese and margarine in a bowl and mix well. Spread evenly over the bottom of an 8 x 8-inch baking dish coated with nonstick cooking spray. Sprinkle ½ of the mozzarella cheese over the pasta layer. Spoon the Classico di Abruzzi Italian Sausage with Peppers & Onions Pasta Sauce evenly over the cheese. Bake at 350°F for 30 minutes. Sprinkle with the remaining mozzarella cheese. Bake for 5 minutes or until the cheese melts. Let stand for 5 minutes. Cut into squares and serve.

SICILIAN PASTA

MAKES 4 SERVINGS

12 ounces bow tie pasta

1 small eggplant,
chopped (about 3 cups)

1 red bell pepper, cut into strips

1 onion, cut into wedges

2 tablespoons olive oil

1 (26-ounce) jar Classico®
di Sicilia Mushrooms &
Ripe Olives Pasta Sauce

Cook the pasta using the package directions; drain.
Set aside and keep warm.

Cook the eggplant, bell pepper and onion in the olive
oil in a large skillet over medium heat until tender.
Add the Classico di Sicilia Mushrooms & Ripe Olives
Pasta Sauce. Simmer for 10 minutes. Serve with
hot pasta.

TORTELLINI
PRIMAVERA

MAKES 4 TO 6 SERVINGS

From Catherine Duffy

1 cup sliced mushrooms

½ cup chopped onion

1 garlic clove, minced

2 tablespoons butter or margarine

1 (10-ounce) package
frozen chopped spinach,
thawed and drained

8 ounces cream cheese, softened

1 tomato, chopped

¾ cup milk

¼ cup grated Parmesan cheese

¼ teaspoon salt

¼ teaspoon pepper

9 ounces cheese tortellini,
cooked and drained

Sauté the mushrooms, onion and garlic in the butter in a skillet. Add the spinach, cream cheese, tomato, milk, Parmesan cheese, salt and pepper and mix well. Cook just until the mixture begins to boil, stirring occasionally. Stir in the tortellini. Cook until heated through. Serve immediately.

"I like to eat this when I want a meatless meal. It also goes great with something off the grill, or it can be eaten as a meal in itself."

ROGER DUFFY

CHICKEN
PARMESAN

MAKES 4 SERVINGS

12 ounces fettuccine

¼ cup dry Italian seasoned bread crumbs

¼ cup (1 ounce) grated Parmesan cheese

1 egg

2 tablespoons water

1 pound boneless skinless chicken breast tenderloins

2 tablespoons olive oil

1 (26-ounce) jar Classico® di Parma Four Cheese Pasta Sauce

Cook the fettuccine using the package directions; drain. Set aside and keep warm.

Combine the bread crumbs and Parmesan cheese in a shallow dish and mix well. Combine the egg and water in a shallow dish and mix well. Dip the chicken in the egg mixture and then the bread crumb mixture. Heat the olive oil in a skillet over medium-high heat. Add the chicken. Cook for 6 to 8 minutes or until brown on both sides and cooked through. Pour the Classico di Parma Four Cheese Pasta Sauce into a saucepan. Cook until heated through.

Divide the fettuccine evenly among four plates. Spoon half of the sauce over the fettuccine. Arrange the chicken over the sauce. Spoon the remaining sauce over the chicken.

CLASSIC
STUFFED SHELLS

MAKES 4 SERVINGS

12 ounces jumbo shells
(about 18 shells)

⅔ cup chopped onion

1 garlic clove, chopped

2 tablespoons olive oil

1 (26-ounce) jar
Classico® di Capri Sun-Dried
Tomato Pasta Sauce

1 (15-ounce) container
ricotta cheese

1 cup (4 ounces)
shredded mozzarella cheese

½ cup (2 ounces)
grated Parmesan cheese

1 egg

1 cup (4 ounces) shredded
mozzarella cheese

Cook the shells using the package directions; drain.

Sauté the onion and garlic in the olive oil in a skillet. Stir in the Classico di Capri Sun-Dried Tomato Pasta Sauce.

Combine the ricotta cheese, 1 cup mozzarella cheese, Parmesan cheese and egg in a bowl and mix well. Stuff the shells with the cheese mixture.

Pour half the pasta sauce evenly over the bottom of a 9 x 13-inch baking dish. Arrange the stuffed shells in the sauce. Pour the remaining sauce over the shells. Bake, covered, at 350°F for 30 minutes. Remove the cover. Sprinkle with 1 cup mozzarella cheese. Bake for 5 minutes or until the cheese melts.

PORK MEDALLIONS
ARRABBIATA

MAKES 8 SERVINGS

8 ounces penne rigate pasta

1 onion, cut into wedges

½ green bell pepper, cut into strips

½ red bell pepper, cut into strips

2 tablespoons olive oil

1 pound pork tenderloin, cut into ½-inch slices

2 garlic cloves, finely chopped

1 (26-ounce) jar Classico® di Roma Arrabbiata Spicy Red Pepper Pasta Sauce

¼ teaspoon thyme leaves

Cook the pasta using the package directions; drain. Set aside and keep warm.

Cook the onion and bell peppers in hot olive oil in a skillet until tender, stirring frequently. Remove the vegetables from the skillet and set aside. Add the pork and garlic to the hot oil. Cook until the pork is browned on both sides. Add the Classico di Roma Arrabbiata Spicy Red Pepper Pasta Sauce and thyme. Bring to a simmer. Simmer for 10 minutes or until the pork is tender, stirring occasionally. Add the vegetables. Cook until heated through. Serve with the hot pasta.

PASTITSO

MAKES 12 SERVINGS

From Louis Spanos

MEAT SAUCE

1 onion, chopped

1 garlic clove, minced

2 tablespoons butter

1 to 1½ pounds ground beef
or lean ground pork

1 (8-ounce) can tomato sauce

½ cup water

1 beef bouillon cube

3 tablespoons fresh parsley

¼ cup red wine (optional)

Salt and pepper to taste

¼ teaspoon cinnamon

½ cup (2 ounces)
grated Parmesan cheese

CREAM SAUCE

6 tablespoons cornstarch

Salt and pepper to taste

1 teaspoon sugar

1 egg, beaten

6 cups cold milk

1 tablespoon butter

½ cup (2 ounces)
grated Parmesan cheese

PASTA

12 ounces macaroni,
pastitso noodles or ziti

Salt

4 to 8 tablespoons
grated Parmesan cheese

FOR THE MEAT SAUCE, sauté the onion and garlic in the butter in a skillet until golden brown. Add the ground beef or lean ground pork. Cook until the ground meat is brown and crumbly, stirring frequently. Add the tomato sauce, water, bouillon cube, parsley, wine, salt and pepper and mix well. Cook for 3 to 5 minutes. Remove from the heat. Stir in the cinnamon and Parmesan cheese.

FOR THE CREAM SAUCE, combine the cornstarch, salt, pepper, sugar, egg and milk in a saucepan and mix until smooth. Bring to a boil over low heat, stirring constantly. Cook until the mixture is smooth and thick, stirring constantly. Remove from the heat. Add the butter and Parmesan cheese, stirring until the butter melts.

FOR THE PASTA, bring a large stockpot of water to a boil. Add a small amount of salt. Add the macaroni. Cook for 10 minutes or until al dente. Drain and rinse with cold water.

To assemble, layer ½ of the macaroni, the meat sauce, the remaining macaroni and the cream sauce in a greased 9 x 13-inch baking pan, sprinkling 1 to 2 tablespoons Parmesan cheese between the layers and over the top. Bake at 350°F for 25 to 30 minutes or until golden brown. Let stand for 20 minutes.

"This entrée is a traditional Greek dinner. We like to make it when our family gets together. It goes well with Greek salad, feta cheese, olives, and pita."

LOUIS SPANOS

CREAMY
CROCKPOT CHICKEN

MAKES 4 TO 6 SERVINGS

From Jaimee Hoke

"Creamy Chicken makes a terrific dinner after a long day. The taste is delicious, and the food just slides down your throat. Don't miss out on this great meal!"

CHRIS HOKE

8 boneless chicken breasts, cut into strips

6 tablespoons butter

1 envelope dry Italian dressing seasoning mix

Freshly cracked pepper to taste

8 ounces cream cheese

1 (10-ounce) can cream of mushroom soup

Cooked peas

Chopped red bell pepper

Combine the chicken, butter, seasoning mix and pepper in a crockpot (slow cooker). Cook on High for 3 hours. Add the cream cheese and soup. Cook 45 minutes or until the cheese melts and a sauce forms. Stir gently. Spoon onto plates. Top with peas and bell pepper. You may serve this over wild rice pilaf.

WILD RICE
TURKEY DRESSING

MAKES 6 SERVINGS

From Willy Robinson

2 (6-ounce) packages
long grain and wild rice mix

¼ cup (½ stick) butter

6 ounces Canadian bacon,
chopped

½ cup sliced green onions

1 garlic clove, minced

¼ cup dry white wine

¼ cup finely chopped
fresh parsley

1 cup chopped walnuts

Prepare the rice mixes using the package directions.
Set aside.

Heat the butter in a large skillet until melted.
Add the bacon, green onions and garlic. Cook for
5 minutes or until the bacon is golden brown and the
onion is tender, stirring constantly. Stir in the wine
and parsley. Add the bacon mixture and walnuts to
the prepared rice and mix well.

Stuff a turkey with the dressing and roast as directed
for the turkey. Spoon any remaining dressing into a
baking dish. Bake, covered, at 350°F for 30 minutes.

"This is an
old family side dish.
We use it for
holidays primarily,
but we also serve
it at BBQ's and
group functions.
It's easy to make and
it fills your home
with terrific aromas.
We hope you enjoy
it as much as we do."

WILLY
ROBINSON

Sweet Potato
Casserole

MAKES 6 TO 8 SERVINGS

From Alan Faneca

"This has quickly become a holiday favorite of mine. When my wife, Julie, first introduced it to me, I didn't know what to make of it. Once I tried it, I was running back for seconds."

ALAN FANECA

SWEET POTATOES OR YAMS
2 cans sweet potatoes or yams, drained
¾ cup (1½ sticks) butter, melted
1 tablespoon vanilla extract
1 teaspoon cinnamon
1 cup sugar
2 eggs

TOPPING
1 cup flour
1 cup packed brown sugar
½ cup (1 stick) butter, melted
1 cup chopped pecans

Mash the sweet potatoes or yams in a bowl. Add the butter, vanilla, cinnamon, sugar and eggs and mix well. Spread evenly over the bottom of a greased 9 x 9-inch baking dish.

FOR THE TOPPING, combine the flour, brown sugar, butter and pecans in a bowl and mix well. Sprinkle evenly over the mixture; the topping should be at least ¼-inch thick.

Bake at 350°F for 30 to 45 minutes or until the mixture is heated through and the topping begins to brown.

SPINACH
MADELINE

MAKES 6 TO 8 SERVINGS

From Barbara Archer

2 packages frozen chopped spinach

¼ cup (½ stick) butter

2 tablespoons chopped onion

2 tablespoons flour

½ cup evaporated milk

½ teaspoon black pepper

¾ teaspoon celery salt

¾ teaspoon garlic salt

1 teaspoon Heinz Worcestershire Sauce

Salt to taste

Red pepper to taste

1 (6-ounce) jar Cheez Whiz® with jalapeño chiles

Buttered bread crumbs (optional)

Cook the spinach using the package directions. Drain, reserving ½ cup of the liquid.

Heat the butter in a saucepan over low heat until melted. Add the onions and cook until tender. Add the flour and stir until smooth; do not brown. Add the milk and reserved spinach liquid gradually, stirring constantly. Cook until smooth and thick, stirring constantly. Add the black pepper, celery salt, garlic salt, Heinz Worcestershire Sauce, salt, red pepper and Cheez Whiz. Cook until the cheese is melted, stirring constantly. Add the cooked spinach and mix well. Spoon into a serving dish and sprinkle with bread crumbs.

You may serve the spinach immediately, but for enhanced flavor chill, covered, for 8 to 12 hours. If refrigerated, bake at 350°F until heated through.

"One of our favorite Southern dishes! Spinach Madeline is sure to please all your guests."

MIKE ARCHER

SPICY POTATO WEDGES
WITH BBQ BEAN & CHEESE DIP

½ (32-ounce) package
Ore-Ida® Country Style Seasoned
Potato Wedges or Ore-Ida®
Zesties!® French Fried Potatoes

1 (16-ounce) can
baked beans, drained

1 cup (4 ounces) shredded
sharp Cheddar cheese

¼ cup Jack Daniel's®
Tennessee Hickory Mesquite™
Grilling Sauce

¼ to ½ teaspoon
hot pepper sauce, or to taste

Prepare the Ore-Ida Country Style Seasoned Potato Wedges or Ore-Ida Zesties! French Fried Potatoes using the package directions.

Puree the beans in a food processor or blender. Pour into a saucepan. Add the cheese, Jack Daniel's Tennessee Hickory Mesquite Grilling Sauce and hot pepper sauce and mix well. Cook over medium heat until heated through. Serve warm with the potatoes. You may heat the dip in a microwave-safe bowl on High for 3 minutes instead.

Charles Reichblum's
Baked Beans

MAKES 3 SERVINGS

1 small onion, chopped

1 (16-ounce) can
Heinz Vegetarian Beans

⅓ cup Heinz Kick'rs™
Hot & Spicy Flavored Ketchup

3 tablespoons brown sugar

Combine the onion, Heinz Vegetarian Beans, Heinz Kick'rs Hot & Spicy Flavored Ketchup and brown sugar in a bowl and mix well. Spoon evenly into a baking dish. Bake, covered, at 400°F for 25 minutes or until hot and bubbly around the edges.

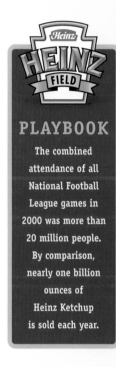

PLAYBOOK

The combined attendance of all National Football League games in 2000 was more than 20 million people. By comparison, nearly one billion ounces of Heinz Ketchup is sold each year.

BAKED HASH BROWN
POTATOES

MAKES 8 SERVINGS

From Jeff Hartings

"This is a
perfect complement
to a juicy steak,
filet or
chicken entree."

JEFF
HARTINGS

2 pounds Ore-Ida®
Frozen Hash Brown Potatoes

1 onion, chopped (optional)

1 (10-ounce) can
cream of chicken soup

2 cups sour cream

½ cup (1 stick) butter,
melted

8 ounces (2 cups)
Cheddar cheese, shredded

Salt and pepper to taste

2 cups crushed potato chips

Place the Ore-Ida Frozen Hash Brown Potatoes in a
large bowl. Let stand for 30 minutes. Add the onion,
soup, sour cream, butter, Cheddar cheese, salt and
pepper and mix well. Spoon evenly into a 9 x 13-inch
baking pan. Sprinkle the potato chips over the top.
Bake at 375°F for 1 hour.

LOUISIANA
PRALINE YAMS

MAKES 6 TO 8 SERVINGS

From Shawn and Tim Lewis

YAMS
3 cups cooked yams
½ cup sugar
2 eggs, beaten
½ teaspoon salt
1½ teaspoons vanilla extract
1 teaspoon cinnamon
½ cup (or less) milk

TOPPING
1 cup packed brown sugar
½ cup flour
¼ cup (½ stick) butter
1 cup chopped pecans

FOR THE YAMS, puree the yams, sugar, eggs, salt, vanilla, cinnamon and enough milk to make the desired consistency in a food processor or mixing bowl. Pour into a greased 9-inch square baking dish.

FOR THE TOPPING, combine the brown sugar and flour in a small bowl. Cut in the butter until crumbly. Stir in the pecans. Sprinkle over the top of the yam mixture.

Bake at 350°F for 20 to 25 minutes.

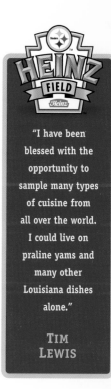

"I have been blessed with the opportunity to sample many types of cuisine from all over the world. I could live on praline yams and many other Louisiana dishes alone."

TIM LEWIS

Sweet-and-Sour Chicken

MAKES 4 SERVINGS

1 pound boneless skinless chicken breasts, cut into ⅔-inch squares

MARINADE
½ teaspoon salt
1½ teaspoons soy sauce
1 tablespoon cornstarch
1 tablespoon cold water

BATTER
½ cup chicken coating mix
½ cup ice water
1 egg yolk
½ cup Sweet-and-Sour Sauce (below)

ASSEMBLY
¼ cup chicken broth
¼ cup water
½ teaspoon cornstarch
6 cups vegetable oil for deep frying
1 green bell pepper, cut into 1-inch pieces
1 carrot, sliced
4 slices canned or fresh pineapple, cut into 1-inch pieces (optional)

SWEET-AND-SOUR SAUCE
1½ cups Heinz Tomato Ketchup
⅔ cup packed brown sugar
⅔ cup sugar
2 slices gingerroot
Juice of 1 lemon

FOR THE MARINADE, combine the salt, soy sauce, 1 tablespoon cornstarch and cold water in a shallow dish and mix well. Add the chicken and toss gently to coat. Marinate for 30 minutes; drain.

FOR THE BATTER, combine the chicken coating mix, ice water and egg yolk in a bowl and mix well. Combine the sweet-and-sour sauce, chicken broth, water and ½ teaspoon cornstarch in a separate bowl and mix well.

TO ASSEMBLE, heat the oil in a wok to 350°F. Reduce the heat to medium. Dip the chicken pieces in the coating mixture. Place in the hot oil a few pieces at a time. Cook for 3 minutes or until browned. Remove and set aside. Repeat with the remaining chicken pieces. Heat the oil to 400°F. Add the chicken to the oil all at once and cook until crisp and cooked through. Remove and set aside.

Remove and discard the oil in the wok, reserving 2 tablespoons. Reduce the heat to medium. Add the bell pepper and carrot and stir-fry. Add the sweet-and-sour mixture. Stir in the pineapple. Cook until the sauce thickens. Remove from the heat and stir in the chicken.

SWEET-AND-SOUR SAUCE Combine the Heinz Tomato Ketchup, brown sugar, sugar, gingerroot and lemon juice in a saucepan. Bring to a boil over low heat. Cook for 20 to 30 minutes, stirring occasionally. Remove and discard the gingerroot. Let stand until cool.

QUICK STIR-FRY BEEF
WITH 3 HEINZ SAUCES

MAKES 4 SERVINGS

1 pound flank, sirloin
or other cut of steak

1 teaspoon chopped gingerroot

½ teaspoon pepper

1 ounce red wine or vermouth

2 tablespoons vegetable oil

1 tablespoon cornstarch

2 tablespoons vegetable oil

½ teaspoon sesame oil

1 teaspoon minced garlic

2 onions, chopped

¼ cup Heinz Tomato Ketchup
or Heinz Kick'rs™ Hot & Spicy
Flavored Ketchup

¼ cup Heinz 57 Sauce

¼ cup Heinz
Worcestershire Sauce

Cilantro (for garnish)

Green onions (for garnish)

Slice the steak into 2 x 2-inch pieces. Combine the gingerroot, pepper, wine, 2 tablespoons vegetable oil and cornstarch in a shallow dish and mix well. Add the steak, stirring to coat. Marinate in the refrigerator for 30 to 60 minutes.

Combine 2 tablespoons vegetable oil, sesame oil and garlic in a hot skillet. Cook until the garlic begins to brown. Add the onions. Add the steak and stir-fry to the desired degree of doneness. Stir in the Heinz Tomato Ketchup or Heinz Kick'rs Hot & Spicy Flavored Ketchup, Heinz 57 Sauce and Heinz Worcestershire Sauce quickly and vigorously. Garnish with cilantro and green onions. Serve immediately.

TERIYAKI CHICKEN
WITH STICKY RICE

MAKES 4 SERVINGS

From Julie Faneca

2 cups rice

Dash of sesame oil

3 tablespoons vegetable oil

4 large boneless chicken breasts, cut into slices

1 bottle thick teriyaki marinade

3 tablespoons sesame seeds, toasted

2 packages frozen chopped broccoli

1 large onion, coarsely chopped

Salt and pepper to taste

Toasted salted cashews

Prepare the rice using the package directions. Set aside and keep warm.

Heat the sesame oil and vegetable oil in a skillet. Add the chicken and cook until cooked through; drain. Return the chicken to the skillet. Pour the marinade over the chicken. Sprinkle the sesame seeds over the chicken.

Cook the broccoli using the package directions. Spray a skillet with nonstick cooking spray. Add the onion. Sprinkle with salt and pepper. Sauté until the onion is tender.

Layer the rice, broccoli, onion and chicken evenly in 4 individual serving bowls. Spoon any remaining sauce from the chicken over the layers. Garnish with cashews. Serve immediately.

"Healthy, delicious, and you can easily adjust the recipe for your taste. This is a favorite of mine during off-season training."

ALAN FANECA

SHRIMP WITH
SNOW PEAS

⅔ pound fresh shrimp

MARINADE
1½ teaspoons rice wine
or dry sherry
½ teaspoon salt
½ teaspoon minced gingerroot
1 tablespoon minced garlic
1½ teaspoons cornstarch
⅛ teaspoon white pepper
1 teaspoon sesame oil

SEASONING SAUCE
1 tablespoon chicken broth
3 tablespoons water
½ teaspoon cornstarch
5 tablespoons
Heinz Tomato Ketchup

ASSEMBLY
½ cup vegetable oil
1 garlic clove, crushed
¼ teaspoon salt
8 ounces fresh snow peas,
or 1 medium onion, sliced

Peel, devein and rinse the shrimp. Pat dry with paper towels.

FOR THE MARINADE, combine the rice wine, ½ teaspoon salt, gingerroot, garlic, 1½ teaspoons cornstarch, white pepper and sesame oil in a shallow dish and mix well. Add the shrimp and toss gently to coat. Marinate for 30 minutes. Drain and pat dry with paper towels.

FOR THE SAUCE, combine the chicken broth, water, ½ teaspoon cornstarch and Heinz Tomato Ketchup in a bowl and mix well.

TO ASSEMBLE, heat the oil in a wok over high heat. Stir-fry the garlic until golden brown. Add the shrimp and stir-fry until pink. Remove the shrimp from the wok. Add ¼ teaspoon salt and the snow peas to the hot oil. Stir-fry for 30 seconds. Add the ketchup mixture. Cook until the sauce thickens. Add the shrimp. Cook until the shrimp are coated with sauce.

TWO-MINUTE WARNING

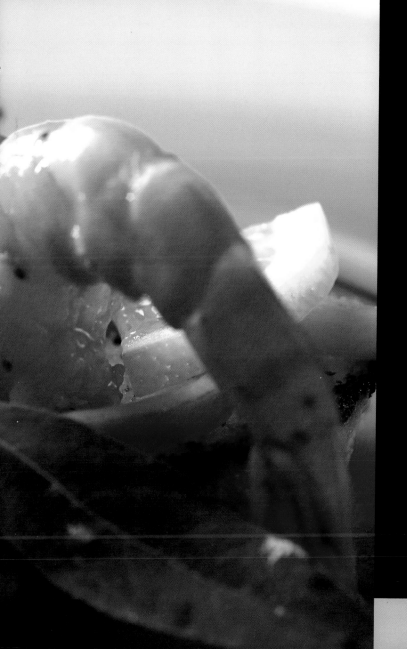

SURPRISE 'EM with something they've never seen before. It's your call – and every dish is as great as a game-winning Hail Mary pass, straight into the hands of your favorite wide receiver, just as the clock runs out.

Sack 'Em
Salsa and Chips

MAKES ABOUT 3 CUPS

2 cups finely chopped eggplant
1 cup finely chopped zucchini
1 cup finely chopped
red bell pepper
1 cup finely chopped
green bell pepper
2 large garlic cloves, minced
2 tablespoons olive oil
1 large tomato, chopped
2 tablespoons Heinz
Apple Cider Vinegar
1 teaspoon salt
½ teaspoon coarsely
ground pepper
1 tablespoon basil
1 teaspoon thyme
½ teaspoon sugar

Sauté the eggplant, zucchini, bell peppers and garlic in the olive oil in a skillet for 8 minutes. Add the tomato, Heinz Apple Cider Vinegar, salt, pepper, basil, thyme and sugar. Cook for 4 to 5 minutes or until the vegetables are tender-crisp. Let stand until cool. Pour the mixture into a glass or plastic container. Chill, covered, for up to 7 days. Serve with pita chips.

GRIDIRON
POTATO DIP

MAKES 3 CUPS

2 cups packed frozen Ore-Ida® Mashed Potatoes

1 cup milk

½ cup chopped plum tomatoes

½ cup chopped red bell pepper, orange bell pepper or yellow bell pepper, or a combination of colors

¼ cup chopped kalamata olives or black olives

¼ cup chopped red onion or chives

½ cup light or regular ranch-style salad dressing

¼ teaspoon salt, or to taste

¼ teaspoon freshly ground pepper, or to taste

Combine the Ore-Ida Mashed Potatoes with the milk in a microwave-safe dish. Microwave for 6 minutes. Combine the prepared potatoes, tomatoes, bell peppers, olives, red onion, salad dressing, salt and pepper in a bowl and mix well. Chill, covered, for 2 hours. Serve with pita chips or bagel chips and fresh vegetables, such as bell pepper wedges, carrot sticks and celery sticks.

You may combine the potatoes and milk in a saucepan instead. Cook for 3 to 4 minutes or until heated through.

PLAYBOOK

The son of former Cincinnati Bengals head coach "Tiger" Johnson has grown up to coach a pretty big team of his own – he's William R. Johnson, the current Chairman, President and Chief Executive Officer of H.J. Heinz Co.

FAST
FOOTBALL FRANKS

MAKES 12 TO 15 SERVINGS

PLAYBOOK

The Heinz Field turf, courtesy of an underground heating unit, is maintained at a constant 62 degrees Fahrenheit.

1 cup Heinz Tomato Ketchup
1 (8-ounce) can crushed pineapple in juice
½ cup grape jelly
1 to 2 tablespoons chopped jalapeño chiles
1 pound cocktail franks

Combine the Heinz Tomato Ketchup, undrained pineapple, jelly and jalapeño chiles in a saucepan. Cook over medium heat until the jelly is melted, stirring constantly. Add the cocktail franks. Cook until the cocktail franks are heated through, stirring occasionally. Serve warm with cocktail picks.

HEINZ
"TK" TACOZ

MAKES 5 SERVINGS

1 pound ground turkey
or ground beef

1 envelope
taco seasoning mix

½ cup water

½ cup Heinz Tomato Ketchup

10 taco shells

Shredded lettuce

Chopped tomatoes

Shredded Cheddar cheese

Sour cream

Brown the ground turkey or ground beef in a skillet, stirring until crumbly; drain. Stir in the taco seasoning mix and water. Simmer for 2 minutes or until slightly thickened, stirring occasionally. Stir in the Heinz Tomato Ketchup. Cook until heated through, stirring occasionally. Spoon the mixture into the taco shells. Top with lettuce, tomatoes, Cheddar cheese and sour cream.

NY DELI WRAPS

MAKES 4 SERVINGS

PLAYBOOK

Completed in 2001
at a cost of
$230 million,
Heinz Field contains
48,000 cubic yards
of concrete;
12,000 tons of
structural steel;
eight tons worth of
giant Heinz Ketchup
bottles, and
approximately
5,000 tons worth
of screaming
football fans.

2 cups prepared creamy coleslaw

2 tablespoons Heinz
Spicy Brown Mustard

3 to 4 tablespoons prepared
white horseradish, drained

3 tablespoons
chopped fresh thyme

4 (10-inch) flour tortillas

1 pound rare roast beef,
sliced thin

2 (7-ounce) jars roasted
red peppers, drained and sliced

1 cup chopped green onions

Combine the coleslaw, Heinz Spicy Brown Mustard, horseradish and thyme in a bowl and mix well. Grill the tortillas over medium-hot coals until soft. Spread the coleslaw mixture on the tortillas to within 1 inch of the edge. Layer the roast beef and red peppers over the coleslaw mixture. Sprinkle with the green onions. Roll to enclose the filling and secure with a wooden pick. Cut the tortillas in half at an angle.

Chill, wrapped in plastic wrap, in a cooler filled with ice until ready to tailgate. Serve with Ore-Ida Fried Onion Rings and Heinz Tomato Ketchup.

CRUDITÉS & GRILLED
KIELBASA WITH HOT SAUCE

SERVES 8 AS AN APPETIZER

3 pounds cooked kielbasa
Kale

CRUDITÉS
Broccoli, chopped
Carrots, julienned
Cauliflower, julienned
Celery, julienned
Jicama, julienned
Grape tomatoes

HOT SAUCE
1½ cups Heinz Chili Sauce
2 tablespoons Heinz
Apple Cider Vinegar
⅓ cup apple jelly
2 tablespoons Heinz
Worcestershire Sauce
1 tablespoon hot sauce
1 tablespoon dry mustard
Cayenne pepper to taste

FOR THE KIELBASA, grill over medium-hot coals until brown and heated through. Cut into chunks. Line a serving platter with kale. Arrange the kielbasa in the center of the serving platter. Spear each piece of kielbasa with a wooden pick.

FOR THE CRUDITÉS, arrange broccoli, carrots, cauliflower, celery, jicama and grape tomatoes around the kielbasa on the serving platter.

FOR THE HOT SAUCE, combine the Heinz Chili Sauce, Heinz Apple Cider Vinegar, jelly, Heinz Worcestershire Sauce, hot sauce, dry mustard and cayenne pepper in a bowl and mix well. Adjust the seasonings to taste. Pour into a serving bowl.

RAGIN' CAJUN
BARBECUED SHRIMP

MAKES 4 SERVINGS

½ cup (1 stick) butter

Hot sauce to taste

Juice of 1 lemon

2 tablespoons Heinz
Worcestershire Sauce

5 large garlic cloves, minced

2 teaspoons freshly
ground black pepper

Cayenne pepper to taste

⅛ teaspoon salt, or to taste

2 pounds (15- to 20-count)
fresh shrimp, peeled and
deveined but with tails left intact

Heinz Worcestershire
Sauce to taste

Hot sauce to taste

Melt the butter in a saucepan over medium heat. Add hot sauce, lemon juice, 2 tablespoons Heinz Worcestershire Sauce, garlic, black pepper, cayenne pepper and salt and mix well. Cook over medium heat until heated through, stirring occasionally.

Combine the lemon juice mixture and the shrimp in a shallow dish and stir to coat well. Chill, covered, for at least 1 hour. Then drain and let the shrimp stand at room temperature for 20 minutes.

Place the shrimp on an oiled grill rack. Grill over medium-hot coals for 4 minutes or until opaque with light brown edges, turning once. Serve immediately with additional Worcestershire sauce and hot sauce.

CREOLE SAUCE

MAKES 1¼ CUPS

1 medium onion,
cut into halves and thinly sliced

¼ cup chopped green
bell pepper

1 tablespoon butter
or margarine

½ cup Heinz Tomato Ketchup

1 tablespoon Heinz
Worcestershire Sauce

2 tablespoons water

Dash of hot pepper sauce

¼ teaspoon salt

Pepper to taste

Combine the onion, bell pepper and butter in a
2-cup microwave-safe measure. Microwave on
High for 2 to 3 minutes or until the vegetables are
tender. Stir in the Heinz Tomato Ketchup, Heinz
Worcestershire Sauce, water, hot pepper sauce, salt
and pepper. Microwave on High for 3 to 4 minutes
or until the flavors blend, stirring twice. Serve over
meat patties, fish or omelets. The microwave oven
used to test this recipe was 650 watts.

You may instead sauté the onion and bell pepper in
the butter in a saucepan on the stove top. Stir in the
remaining ingredients and simmer, uncovered, for
10 minutes, stirring occasionally.

FOR TUNA CREOLE, drain and flake a 6½-ounce can of
tuna and add to the sauce before heating. Serve over
hot buttered rice.

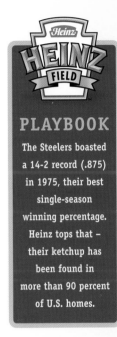

PLAYBOOK

The Steelers boasted
a 14-2 record (.875)
in 1975, their best
single-season
winning percentage.
Heinz tops that –
their ketchup has
been found in
more than 90 percent
of U.S. homes.

CHILI
ITALIANO

MAKES 6 SERVINGS

1 cup medium shell pasta

1 pound lean ground beef

¾ cup chopped onion

1 (26-ounce) jar
Classico® di Napoli Tomato
& Basil Pasta Sauce

2 cups water

1 (4-ounce) can sliced
mushrooms, drained

2 ounces sliced pepperoni

1 tablespoon Wyler's® Beef Flavor
Instant Bouillon & Seasoning

1 tablespoon chili powder

Cook the pasta using the package directions; drain. Brown the ground beef with the onion in a skillet, stirring until the ground beef is crumbly; drain. Stir in the Classico di Napoli Tomato & Basil Pasta Sauce, water, mushrooms, pepperoni, Wyler's Beef Flavor Instant Bouillon Granules and chili powder. Bring to a boil. Reduce the heat. Simmer for 20 minutes. Stir in the pasta shells.

FINGER BLITZIN'
BBQ RIBS

MAKES 6 SERVINGS

PLAYBOOK

Those diamond-shaped doohickeys you see hanging around Heinz Field are called "Cycloids," similar to the "hypocycloid" patterns from the "Steelmark" logo on the Steelers' helmets.

RUB
1 tablespoon brown sugar
1 tablespoon paprika
1 tablespoon salt
1 tablespoon pepper
1 teaspoon garlic powder
1 teaspoon onion powder

RIBS
3 racks baby-back ribs
1 cup bourbon
Jack Daniel's® Sizzling Smokehouse Blend™ Grilling Sauce

FOR THE RUB, combine the brown sugar, paprika, salt, pepper, garlic powder and onion powder in a bowl and mix well.

FOR THE RIBS, place the ribs in a shallow pan. Pour the bourbon over the ribs. Marinate in the refrigerator for 30 minutes, turning the ribs several times; drain. Sprinkle the ribs with ⅔ of the rub. Let stand for 30 minutes.

Place the ribs in a roasting pan. Roast, uncovered, at 350°F for 30 minutes. Grill over medium-hot coals until brown and cooked through, brushing frequently with the Jack Daniel's Sizzling Smokehouse Blend Grilling Sauce. Sprinkle with the remaining rub. Serve with additional grilling sauce on the side.

FIRST & GOAL
FLANK STEAK

MAKES 4 TO 6 SERVINGS

1½ pounds flank steak
½ cup Jack Daniel's®
Tennessee Hickory Mesquite™
Grilling Sauce
¼ cup red wine

Place the steak in a sealable heavy-duty plastic bag. Mix the Jack Daniel's Tennessee Hickory Mesquite Grilling Sauce and wine in a bowl. Pour the mixture over the steak and seal the plastic bag. Marinate in the refrigerator for 4 to 24 hours, turning the bag several times to coat the steak. Discard the marinade. Grill the steak over medium-hot coals to the desired degree of doneness, turning once and brushing with additional grilling sauce.

TWICE BLITZED
POTATOES

MAKES 2 SERVINGS

1 package frozen Ore-Ida®
Twice Baked Potatoes

Wrap each Ore-Ida Twice Baked Potato in foil. Place the potatoes filling side up on a grill rack. Grill over medium-hot coals for 30 to 40 minutes or until heated through.

CHILI RUBBED CHICKEN
WITH DEFENSE DIP

MAKES 6 SERVINGS

CHILI RUB

¾ cup chili powder

3 tablespoons brown sugar

2 teaspoons cayenne pepper

DEFENSE DIP

1 cup Jack Daniel's®
Original No.7 Barbeque Recipe™
Grilling Sauce

¾ cup Heinz Tomato Ketchup

⅓ cup fresh orange juice

1 tablespoon soy sauce

1 teaspoon hot pepper sauce

2 (3½-pound) chickens,
quartered and backbones
discarded

Salt and pepper to taste

FOR THE RUB, combine the chili powder, brown sugar and cayenne pepper in a bowl and mix well.

FOR THE DIP, combine the Jack Daniel's Original No.7 Barbeque Recipe Grilling Sauce and Heinz Tomato Ketchup in a small bowl and mix well. Stir in the orange juice, soy sauce and hot pepper sauce.

To prepare, season the chicken with salt and pepper. Arrange the chicken in a single layer on a large baking sheet. Sprinkle the rub over both sides of the chicken. Let stand in the refrigerator for 1 hour. Arrange the chicken skin side down on the grill rack away from the direct heat. Close the grill cover. Grill over medium-hot coals for 35 to 40 minutes or until the chicken is cooked through, turning every 5 minutes. The Chili Rub may burn slightly. Serve immediately with the Defense Dip.

CHEDDAR BACON SAUCE
FOR HAMBURGERS

MAKES ¾ CUP

¼ cup crumbled crisp-cooked bacon (about 4 slices bacon)

¼ cup (1 ounce) shredded Cheddar cheese

¼ cup chopped green onions

½ cup Heinz Tomato Ketchup

Combine the bacon, Cheddar cheese, green onions and Heinz Tomato Ketchup in a bowl and mix well. Serve as a sauce for hamburgers.

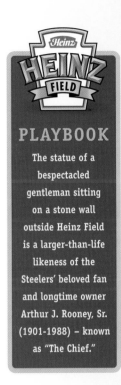

PLAYBOOK

The statue of a bespectacled gentleman sitting on a stone wall outside Heinz Field is a larger-than-life likeness of the Steelers' beloved fan and longtime owner Arthur J. Rooney, Sr. (1901-1988) – known as "The Chief."

TAMPA BAY
SPICY SHRIMP

MAKES 6 SERVINGS

MARINADE
½ cup vegetable oil

¼ cup Heinz Tomato Ketchup

¼ cup Heinz
Apple Cider Vinegar

2 tablespoons Heinz
Worcestershire Sauce

1 tablespoon light brown sugar

½ teaspoon dry mustard

⅛ teaspoon salt, or to taste

3 bay leaves

Hot sauce to taste

SHRIMP
Old Bay® Seasoning to taste

2 pounds shrimp,
peeled and deveined

1 cup sliced onion

FOR THE MARINADE, combine the oil, Heinz Tomato Ketchup, Heinz Apple Cider Vinegar, Heinz Worcestershire Sauce, brown sugar, dry mustard, salt, bay leaves and hot sauce in a bowl and mix well.

FOR THE SHRIMP, fill a 3-quart stockpot with water. Bring the water to a boil and add Old Bay Seasoning. Add the shrimp. Boil for 3 minutes or until the shrimp turn pink; drain. Add the shrimp to the marinade and toss to coat. Add the onion. Chill, covered, for 4 hours. Serve with grilled garlic bread.

SOUTHWESTERN TRICOLOR
TORTELLINI SALAD
WITH BALSAMIC VINAIGRETTE

MAKES 6 TO 8 SERVINGS

SALAD

14 ounces frozen
southwestern-style chicken
strips, thawed

3 pounds tricolor tortellini

8 ounces sun-dried cherries

2 tablespoons
finely chopped fresh basil

BALSAMIC VINAIGRETTE

¼ cup Dijon mustard

¼ cup honey

¾ cup Heinz Balsamic Vinegar

1½ cups olive oil

1 teaspoon kosher salt

¼ teaspoon pepper

FOR THE SALAD, cut the chicken strips into halves. Combine the chicken, tortellini and cherries in a bowl and toss to mix. Stir in the basil.

FOR THE VINAIGRETTE, combine the Dijon mustard and honey in a bowl and whisk until blended. Whisk in the Heinz Balsamic Vinegar gradually. Add the olive oil and whisk to blend. Stir in the salt and pepper.

To assemble, pour the vinaigrette over the salad and toss to combine. Chill, covered, for 1 to 2 hours. Serve cold.

PLAYBOOK

Heinz Field's award-winning design forms a horseshoe-shaped seating bowl with an open South end zone, offering fans a spectacular vista of Pittsburgh's downtown skyline.

PLAY-BY-PLAY
POTATO SALAD

MAKES 6 SERVINGS

PLAYBOOK

When Steelers' current owner Dan Rooney broke ground for Heinz Field in 1999, he used the same shovel with which his dad, Art Rooney, Sr., broke ground for Three Rivers Stadium three decades earlier.

DRESSING

3 tablespoons Heinz Spicy Brown Mustard

⅓ cup Heinz Apple Cider Vinegar

1½ cups extra-virgin olive oil

POTATO SALAD

10 medium red potatoes

½ cup white wine

½ cup Wyler's® Chicken Flavor Instant Bouillon

¼ cup minced fresh parsley

¼ cup minced fresh basil

2 bunches scallions, finely chopped

Salt and freshly ground pepper to taste

½ pound baby French green beans, stems removed

1 (9-ounce) can white albacore tuna

1 cup grape tomatoes, halved

½ cup capers, drained

½ cup chopped red onion

½ cup kalamata olives

6 hard-cooked eggs, peeled and quartered

6 anchovy filets (optional)

FOR THE DRESSING, combine the Heinz Spicy Brown Mustard and Heinz Apple Cider Vinegar in a food processor. Process until mixed. Add the olive oil in a steady stream with the food processor running.

FOR THE SALAD, cook the unpeeled potatoes in water to cover in a large saucepan just until tender; drain. Slice the hot potatoes. Combine the potatoes, wine and Wyler's Chicken Flavor Instant Bouillon in a large bowl and toss to coat. Add the parsley, basil, scallions, salt and pepper and mix well.

Blanch the green beans in boiling salted water in a saucepan until tender-crisp; drain. Plunge the green beans into ice water to stop the cooking process; drain.

Add the green beans, tuna, tomatoes, capers, red onion, olives, eggs and anchovies to the potato mixture and mix well. Serve at room temperature.

GRILLED CRAB
PO' BOYS

MAKES 4 SERVINGS

MUSTARD DRESSING

6 tablespoons chopped
Heinz Sweet Pickles

¼ cup chopped drained capers

4 to 5 tablespoons
Heinz Chili Sauce

1 tablespoon Heinz
Spicy Brown Mustard

CRAB PO' BOYS

8 ounces crab meat, flaked

1½ cups fresh
white bread crumbs

¾ cup mayonnaise

½ cup chopped green onions

1 teaspoon Old Bay® Seasoning

Salt and pepper to taste

1 egg yolk

2 tablespoons Heinz
Spicy Brown Mustard

1 French baguette

FOR THE DRESSING, combine the Heinz Sweet Pickles, capers, Heinz Chili Sauce and Heinz Spicy Brown Mustard in a bowl and mix well. Chill, covered, until needed.

FOR THE PO' BOYS, combine the crab meat, 1 cup of the bread crumbs, mayonnaise, green onions and Old Bay Seasoning in a bowl and mix well. Season with salt and pepper. Add the egg yolk and Heinz Spicy Brown Mustard and mix well. Shape the mixture into 2½-inch patties. Coat the patties with the remaining ½ cup bread crumbs.

Grill the patties over medium-hot coals on a grill rack brushed with oil for 8 minutes or until golden brown, turning once. Cut the baguette into 3- to 4-inch slices. Split each slice in half. Grill for 2 minutes or until lightly toasted, turning once.

To serve, spread the dressing over the baguette slices. Top with the grilled crab meat patties.

Vegetarian Lasagna
Roll-Ups di Napoli

9 lasagna noodles

1 (15-ounce) container ricotta cheese

1 (10-ounce) package frozen chopped spinach, thawed and drained

1 cup (4 ounces) shredded mozzarella cheese

¼ cup (1 ounce) grated Parmesan cheese

1 egg, beaten

1 (26-ounce) jar Classico® di Napoli Tomato & Basil Pasta Sauce

Cook the lasagna noodles using the package directions; drain.

Combine the ricotta cheese, spinach, mozzarella cheese, Parmesan cheese and egg in a bowl and mix well. Spread ⅓ cup over each lasagna noodle. Roll up the noodles.

Pour ⅓ cup Classico di Napoli Tomato & Basil Pasta Sauce evenly over the bottom of a 9 x 13-inch baking dish. Arrange the lasagna rolls seam side down in the sauce. Spoon the remaining sauce over the rolls. Bake, covered, at 350°F for 35 minutes or until hot.

BACKYARD BRAWL
BAKED BEANS

4 slices thick-sliced bacon, chopped

2 cups chopped onions

½ green bell pepper, chopped

2 garlic cloves, chopped

2 (16-ounce) cans Heinz Vegetarian Beans, drained and rinsed

⅓ cup molasses

¼ cup Jack Daniel's® Original No.7 Barbeque Recipe™ Grilling Sauce

¼ cup Heinz Kick'rs™ Hot & Spicy Flavored Ketchup

¼ cup packed brown sugar

1 tablespoon Heinz Worcestershire Sauce

1 teaspoon Heinz Spicy Brown Mustard

1 tablespoon Heinz Apple Cider Vinegar

1 tablespoon dry mustard

¼ tablespoon Liquid Smoke, or to taste

Salt and freshly ground pepper to taste

Cook the bacon in a heavy saucepan over medium heat until the drippings are rendered. Add the onions, bell pepper and garlic. Cook for 5 minutes or until the vegetables are soft. Stir in the Heinz Vegetarian Beans, molasses, Jack Daniel's Original No.7 Barbeque Recipe Grilling Sauce, Heinz Kick'rs Hot & Spicy Flavored Ketchup, brown sugar, Heinz Worcestershire Sauce, Heinz Spicy Brown Mustard, Heinz Apple Cider Vinegar, dry mustard and Liquid Smoke. Simmer, uncovered, for 10 to 15 minutes or until the mixture is thickened and the flavors are blended, stirring occasionally with a wooden spoon. Season with salt and pepper. You may combine the ingredients in a baking dish and bake at 350°F for 30 minutes instead.

FRIED RAVIOLI

WITH TOMATO ROSEMARY SAUCE

MAKES 4 SERVINGS

TOMATO ROSEMARY SAUCE

1 tablespoon olive oil

½ pound plum tomatoes

1 teaspoon minced garlic

Red pepper flakes to taste

1 tablespoon tomato paste

¼ teaspoon rosemary

⅛ teaspoon sugar, or to taste

Salt and pepper to taste

2 tablespoons chopped
fresh Italian parsley

RAVIOLI

1 cup plain bread crumbs

½ cup (2 ounces)
grated Parmesan cheese

⅔ cup evaporated milk

24 cheese ravioli

4 cups corn oil

FOR THE SAUCE, heat the olive oil in a medium sauté pan over low heat. Add the tomatoes, garlic and red pepper flakes. Sauté over medium heat for 10 minutes. Stir in the tomato paste, rosemary, sugar, salt and pepper. Reduce the heat. Simmer for 10 minutes, stirring occasionally. Remove from the heat and stir in the parsley.

FOR THE RAVIOLI, combine the bread crumbs and cheese in a shallow dish. Pour the milk into a shallow dish. Dip the ravioli in the milk. Coat evenly with the bread crumb mixture. Heat the corn oil to 365°F in a deep fryer. Fry the ravioli a few at a time for 2 minutes or until golden brown. Drain on paper towels. Serve immediately with the Tomato Rosemary Sauce. Serve with assorted grilled vegetables and your favorite Heinz sauce for dipping.

VICTORY CELEBRATIONS

YOU'LL MAKE the last

play of the day the sweetest

when you pass these desserts

to everyone on your team.

Victory has never tasted better!

CHOCOLATE CHIP
SOUR CREAM CAKE

MAKES 20 SERVINGS

From Jane Tylski

4 eggs
1 cup sour cream
¾ cup vegetable oil
¾ cup water
½ cup sugar
1 (2-layer) package
yellow cake mix
1 (4-ounce) package
chocolate instant pudding mix
1 cup (6 ounces)
chocolate chips

Preheat oven to 350°F.

Beat the eggs, sour cream, oil, water, sugar, cake mix and pudding mix in a mixing bowl until smooth. Stir in the chocolate chips. Pour into a greased and floured bundt pan. Bake at 350°F for 50 to 60 minutes or until the cake tests done.

Note: To prevent the chocolate chips from sinking to the bottom of the cake during baking, sprinkle with a small amount of flour before adding to the batter.

"This is definitely a dessert to have when the steaks are on the grill."

RICH TYLSKI

CHOCOLATE
ANGEL PIE

MAKES 8 SERVINGS

3 egg whites
¾ cup sugar
½ teaspoon vinegar
¼ teaspoon cinnamon
1 baked (10-inch) pie shell
8 ounces semisweet chocolate
¼ cup hot water
2 cups whipping cream
6 tablespoons
confectioners' sugar
½ teaspoon cinnamon

Preheat oven to 325°F.

Beat the egg whites and sugar in a mixing bowl until soft peaks form. Add the vinegar and cinnamon. Beat until stiff peaks form. Spread over the bottom and up the side of the baked pie shell to form a shell of meringue. Bake at 325°F for 20 minutes. The meringue will puff up and then fall slightly as it cools.

Place the chocolate and hot water in a microwave-safe bowl. Microwave on High until the chocolate melts. Let stand to cool. Spread ½ of the chocolate mixture over the bottom of the meringue.

Whip the cream, confectioners' sugar and cinnamon in a mixing bowl until soft peaks form. Spread ½ of the whipped cream over the chocolate layer in the pie. Add the remaining chocolate mixture to the remaining whipped cream and mix well. Spread over the top of the pie to form a fifth layer. Swirl with a spoon to marbleize. Chill for several hours or until set.

Rum Cake

From Jane Tylski

"Every time
we go
to a pot luck,
this is what
people ask me
to bring."

RICH
TYLSKI

CAKE
½ cup chopped pecans
1 (2-layer) package
butter cake mix
1 (4-ounce) package
vanilla instant pudding mix
¼ cup light rum
½ cup water
½ cup vegetable oil
4 eggs

RUM GLAZE
1 cup sugar
½ cup (1 stick) butter
¼ cup rum
¼ cup water

Preheat oven to 350°F.

FOR THE CAKE, butter and flour a bundt pan. Sprinkle with the pecans. Mix the cake mix and pudding mix in a large mixing bowl. Add the rum, water, oil and eggs. Beat for 2 minutes or until smooth. Pour into the prepared pan. Bake at 350°F for 50 to 60 minutes or until the cake tests done.

FOR THE GLAZE, combine the sugar, butter, rum and water in a saucepan. Boil for 2 to 3 minutes, stirring constantly until smooth.

To assemble, pierce the top of the cake with a fork. Pour the hot glaze over the cake. Let stand for 10 to 15 minutes. Invert onto a cake plate.

CHOCOLATE
KAHLÚA® CHEESECAKE

MAKES 16 SERVINGS

CRUST
1½ cups crushed
chocolate wafers
3 tablespoons butter, melted

FILLING
1 tablespoon (heaping)
instant espresso powder
⅓ cup Kahlúa® coffee liqueur
48 ounces cream cheese,
softened
1¼ cups sugar
5 eggs
1 cup heavy cream
8 ounces semisweet
chocolate, melted

TOPPING
2 cups sour cream
¼ cup granulated sugar

Preheat oven to 350°F.

FOR THE CRUST, mix the crushed chocolate wafers and butter in a bowl. Press into a greased 10-inch springform pan. Chill until needed.

FOR THE FILLING, mix the espresso powder and Kahlúa in a microwave-safe bowl. Microwave on High until the espresso powder dissolves. Beat the cream cheese and sugar in a large mixing bowl until smooth. Add the eggs 1 at a time, beating well after each addition. Add the cream, chocolate and espresso mixture and mix well. Pour into the crust. Bake at 350°F for 50 to 55 minutes. Remove from the oven. Increase the oven temperature to 400°F.

FOR THE TOPPING, beat the sour cream and sugar in a small bowl. Spread over the hot cheesecake. Bake for 5 minutes. Remove from the oven to cool. Chill until serving time.

AMARETTO
BREAD PUDDING

BREAD PUDDING

1 small loaf dry challah bread, cut into cubes

4 cups (1 quart) half-and-half

2 tablespoons butter

3 eggs

1½ cups sugar

2 tablespoons almond extract

1 cup golden raisins

¾ cup sliced almonds

AMARETTO SAUCE

½ cup (1 stick) butter, softened

1 cup confectioners' sugar

1 egg, beaten

¼ cup Amaretto liqueur

FOR THE BREAD PUDDING, place the bread cubes in a medium bowl. Pour the half-and-half over the bread cubes. Let stand for 1 hour.

Preheat oven to 325°F.

Grease a 9 x 13-inch baking dish with the butter. Beat the eggs, sugar and almond extract in a small bowl. Stir into the bread mixture. Fold in the raisins and almonds. Spread evenly in the prepared baking dish. Bake at 325°F on the middle oven rack for 50 minutes or until golden brown. Remove from the oven to cool.

FOR THE SAUCE, combine the butter and confectioners' sugar in a double boiler. Cook over simmering water until the sugar is dissolved and the butter is melted, stirring constantly. Remove from the heat. Add a small amount of the hot mixture to the beaten egg. Whisk the egg into the hot mixture. Cook over the simmering water until thickened, whisking constantly and making sure the pan does not touch the simmering water. Remove from the heat. Stir in the liqueur.

Serve the warm Amaretto sauce over the warm bread pudding.

DIRT
PUDDING

MAKES 10 SERVINGS

From Matt Cushing

⅔ (12-ounce) package
Oreo® cookies, crushed

12 ounces whipped
topping, thawed

8 ounces cream cheese,
softened

¼ cup (½ stick) butter,
softened

1 cup confectioners' sugar

2 (4-ounce) packages
French vanilla
instant pudding mix

3½ cups milk

Spread ½ of the cookie crumbs in a 9 x 13-inch dish. Beat the whipped topping, cream cheese, butter and confectioners' sugar in a mixing bowl until smooth. Spread over the cookie crumb layer.

Combine the pudding mix and milk in a bowl and beat until smooth. Spread over the cream cheese layer. Sprinkle the top with the remaining cookie crumbs. Chill until serving time.

"This is always
a favorite
around our house,
especially with
weekend guests.
The problem is
it never lasts
the whole weekend."

MATT
CUSHING

FALLING CHOCOLATE
CAKE WITH RASPBERRY SAUCE

MAKES SIX 8-OUNCE RAMEKINS

RASPBERRY SAUCE
4 cups fresh or
frozen raspberries
½ cup sugar

CHOCOLATE CAKE
2 tablespoons unsalted butter
2 tablespoons flour
12 ounces semisweet
chocolate, coarsely chopped
1 cup (2 sticks) unsalted butter
1 cup sugar
½ cup flour
6 eggs

ASSEMBLY
4 cups vanilla ice cream
2 tablespoons
confectioners' sugar
6 sprigs of mint

FOR THE RASPBERRY SAUCE, combine the raspberries and sugar in a small saucepan. Bring to a boil over high heat, stirring constantly. Boil until the sugar dissolves. Remove from the heat to cool. Puree ½ of the sauce in a food processor fitted with a steel blade. Combine with the remaining sauce in a bowl and mix well. Chill, covered, in the refrigerator until cold.

Preheat oven to 350°F.

FOR THE CHOCOLATE CAKE, generously butter and flour six 8-ounce ramekins. Heat the chocolate and 1 cup butter in a double boiler over simmering water until melted, stirring constantly. Remove from the heat to cool. Beat the sugar, ½ cup flour and eggs in a large mixing bowl for 5 minutes or until thick and fluffy. Gently beat in the cooled chocolate mixture. Pour into the prepared ramekins, filling ⅔ to ¾ full. Bake at 350°F for 15 minutes or until the cakes begin to puff up.

TO ASSEMBLE AND SERVE, run a knife around the edge of each ramekin to loosen the cake from the side. Invert the warm cakes onto serving plates. Surround each cake with raspberry sauce. Place a scoop of vanilla ice cream beside each cake. Garnish with confectioners' sugar and springs of fresh mint.

STRAWBERRY TIRAMISU

MAKES 8 SERVINGS

**12 ounces light
cream cheese, softened**

¾ cup confectioners' sugar

5 tablespoons Marsala

½ cup sour cream

1 pint strawberries

¾ cup boiling water

2 tablespoons sugar

**2½ teaspoons
instant espresso powder**

2 tablespoons Marsala

**1 (8-ounce) package
ladyfingers**

1 ounce chocolate, grated

Process the cream cheese, confectioners' sugar and 5 tablespoons Marsala in a food processor until smooth. Add the sour cream and mix well.

Cut ½ of the strawberries into slices. Cut the remaining strawberries into halves.

Combine the boiling water, 2 tablespoons of sugar and espresso powder in a medium bowl and stir until dissolved. Stir in 2 tablespoons Marsala.

Dip 1 ladyfinger briefly into the espresso mixture, turning to coat. Place flat side up in an 8 x 8-inch glass dish. Repeat with enough ladyfingers to cover the bottom of the dish, trimming the edges to fit.

Spread ⅔ of the cream cheese mixture over the ladyfingers. Cover with the sliced strawberries. Dip the remaining ladyfingers into the espresso mixture and arrange over the strawberries to cover completely, trimming the edges of the ladyfingers to fit. Spread the remaining cream cheese mixture over the top. Sprinkle with the grated chocolate. Arrange the strawberry halves around the edges.

Chill, covered, for 4 hours or longer before serving.

APPLE COBBLER

MAKES 8 SERVINGS

10 medium apples
1 cup flour
1 cup sugar
½ teaspoon salt
1 egg
⅓ cup butter, melted
1 teaspoon baking powder
Cinnamon-sugar for sprinkling

Preheat oven to 350°F.

Cut the apples into slices. Place in a buttered 9 x 9-inch baking pan. Combine the flour, sugar, salt and egg in a bowl and mix well. Add the butter and mix well. Pat onto the apples. Sprinkle generously with cinnamon-sugar. Bake uncovered at 350°F for 40 minutes.

LOVE APPLE PIE

MAKES ONE 9-INCH PIE

⅓ cup Heinz Tomato Ketchup
2 teaspoons lemon juice
6 cups (about 2 pounds) peeled, sliced tart cooking apples
⅔ cup flour
⅓ cup sugar
1 teaspoon cinnamon
⅓ cup butter or margarine
1 unbaked (9-inch) pie shell

Preheat oven to 425°F.

Blend the Heinz Tomato Ketchup and lemon juice in a large bowl. Add the apples and toss to coat. Mix the flour, sugar and cinnamon in a bowl. Cut in the butter until crumbly. Fill the pie shell with the apple mixture. Sprinkle with the flour mixture. Bake at 425°F for 40 to 45 minutes or until the apples are tender. Serve warm with ice cream if desired.

Note: If the apples are very tart, add 1 to 2 teaspoons sugar to the ketchup mixture.

STRAWBERRY
LEMON CURD TART

MAKES 8 SERVINGS

LEMON CURD FILLING

1½ cups sugar

½ cup (1 stick) unsalted butter, melted and cooled

½ cup fresh lemon juice

3 eggs, beaten

2 egg yolks, beaten

2 tablespoons grated fresh lemon zest

1 (10-inch) tart shell in a pan with a removable bottom, baked

STRAWBERRY TOPPING

4 cups whole fresh strawberries

½ cup strawberry jam

FOR THE FILLING, combine the sugar, butter, lemon juice, eggs, egg yolks and lemon zest in a heavy medium saucepan. Cook over low heat for 10 minutes or until thickened, whisking constantly. Do not boil. Pour into a bowl immediately and lay a piece of plastic wrap directly on the surface. Chill for 3 to 12 hours.

Spoon the lemon filling into the baked tart shell.

FOR THE TOPPING, arrange the strawberries decoratively over the filling. Strain the jam into a saucepan, discarding the solids. Heat until melted, stirring constantly. Brush over the strawberries. Chill for 1 to 6 hours or until the glaze sets. Release the side of the pan and serve.

CARAMEL FUDGE BROWNIES

MAKES APPROXIMATELY 18 TO 24 BROWNIES   *From Traci Bruener*

1 (14-ounce) package caramels
⅓ cup evaporated milk
1 (2-layer) package
German chocolate cake mix
¾ cup (1½ sticks) butter
or margarine, softened
1 cup chopped walnuts
⅓ cup evaporated milk
1 cup (6 ounces) chocolate chips

Preheat oven to 350°F.

Unwrap the caramels and place in a saucepan. Add ⅓ cup evaporated milk. Cook over low heat until the caramels are melted, stirring constantly. Keep warm.

Mix the cake mix, butter, walnuts, and ⅓ cup evaporated milk in a bowl. Press ½ of the mixture into a greased 9 x 13-inch baking pan. Bake at 350°F for 6 minutes. Remove from the oven. Sprinkle with the chocolate chips. Pour the hot caramel mixture over the chocolate chips. Crumble the remaining cake mix mixture over the top. Return to the oven. Bake for 16 minutes. Cool completely before cutting into squares.

Note: This recipe makes very rich, dense brownies so you may want to cut into small squares.

"Seriously to die for!!! The ultimate training camp treat!"

MARK BRUENER

JUMBLEBERRY PIE

1 (2-crust) deep-dish
pie pastry
3 cups blackberries
3 cups blueberries
2½ cups raspberries
⅓ cup cornstarch
1½ cups sugar
¼ cup fresh lemon juice
⅛ teaspoon nutmeg
⅛ teaspoon cinnamon
1 tablespoon butter,
cut into pieces
¼ cup half-and-half
Sugar for sprinkling
Peach ice cream (optional)

Preheat oven to 425°F.

Roll the pie pastry into a 10-inch circle on a lightly floured surface. Fit into a 9-inch deep-dish pie plate, leaving a ½-inch overhang.

Combine the blackberries, blueberries, raspberries, cornstarch, sugar, lemon juice, nutmeg and cinnamon in a large bowl and toss to mix well. Mound into the prepared pie plate. Dot with the butter. Roll the remaining pie pastry into a 13-inch circle on a lightly floured surface. Drape over the top of the pie, leaving a 1-inch overhang. Fold the overhang under the bottom pastry, press the edge to seal, then flute the edge. Brush the pastry with the half-and-half. Cut slits in the top to form vents. Sprinkle lightly with sugar. Place the pie on a baking sheet.

Bake at 425°F on the middle oven rack for 20 minutes. Reduce the oven temperature to 375°F. Bake for 35 to 40 minutes longer or until the crust is golden brown and the filling is bubbly. Serve with peach ice cream if desired.

The majority of the recipes in this cookbook were created by four certified professional chefs and a world-renowned nutritionist who together bring decades of experience to the development of dishes that are both delicious and nutritious. We're pleased to have them playing on the Heinz team!

BYRON J. BARDY

CERTIFIED MASTER CHEF – BARDY FOODSERVICE CONSULTING CO.

In 1981, Chef Bardy received his Master Chef degree from the American Culinary Federation (ACF) Educational Institute. He was one of the first five people nationally to earn certification as a master chef. This status is bestowed upon people who have displayed the highest level of culinary skill and knowledge. Today, Bardy is one of only 57 certified master chefs in the United States, a testament to the fact that achieving such recognition comes through extreme dedication to his craft. Chef Bardy also has numerous local, national and international culinary awards to his credit, including the American Culinary Federation's "President's Gold Medal" in 1991.

Byron J. Bardy

Bardy has taught gourmet cooking classes as well as tallow and ice sculpturing. He is also an approved culinary judge for the American Culinary Federation and the Master Chef examination for The Culinary Institute of America.

Bardy participated in the 2002 Olympic Winter Games. He coordinated the Arts and Culture Dinners for the Salt Lake Organizing Committee in conjunction with the James Beard Foundation's Celebration of Great Chefs. He is an active member of The Research Chefs Association, American Culinary Federation and American Academy of Chefs.

Bardy, now an on-site consultant for H.J. Heinz Company, previously served as national Manager of Foodservice Research and New Business Development for the Heinz Foodservice Division. He and his wife, Judy, own and operate Bardy Foodservice Consulting Company in Pittsburgh, Pennsylvania.

ALAN MCDONALD, C.E.C.
CORPORATE CHEF – HEINZ NORTH AMERICA

Alan McDonald, C.E.C.

In his role as Corporate Chef, Foodservice Culinary Product Development in the Heinz Foodservice Division, Chef McDonald works continually with the nation's top restaurant chains and foodservice companies to develop new and interesting ideas that focus on emerging food trends. In addition to helping Heinz customers, McDonald seeks to continue the growth of the Heinz Foodservice product line. His goal is to provide high-level product research and development, and he works closely with marketing and sales teams to meet customer needs.

Chef McDonald has more than 15 years of culinary experience, including Executive Committee, Corporate Chef, Area Executive Chef, Regional Executive Chef, District Chef, Food Service Director and other management roles. Just prior to joining Heinz in 2002, he was a corporate chef for Brinker International Corner Bakery restaurants. McDonald has also served as the Executive Chef for the largest region in the Sodexho Marriott Corporation, serving 450 units. Chef McDonald also was a panelist on the Society for Food Management on its United States tour and was named 1997 Young Maverick Chef by Restaurant and Institutions magazine.

Chef McDonald earned his Associate of Science in Culinary Arts degree from Johnson & Wales University in Providence, Rhode Island, where he focused on classical, international and Oriental cuisine. He has continued his education at the Culinary Institute of America in New York and California, successfully completing seven advanced programs.

Chef McDonald and his wife live in Colleyville, Texas.

JEFF WAGERS

DEVELOPMENT CHEF – HEINZ FOODSERVICE DIVISION

As Development Chef for the Heinz Foodservice Division, Jeff Wagers is responsible for Foodservice culinary product development and the continued growth of the division's product line. Wagers engages in high-level product research and development and works closely with the division's marketing and sales teams to develop new technologies and flavor concepts based on current industry trends.

Jeff Wagers

Before joining Heinz in April, 2002, Wagers served as corporate chef for Griffith Laboratories in Alsip, Illinois. He joined Griffith in June 1999 and, while there, he used his culinary knowledge and expertise to support research and development scientists with product formulation. He developed and presented new product concepts to food processors, national chain accounts and quick-service restaurants. His duties at Heinz build on that solid foundation to bring exciting new concepts and products to our Foodservice customers.

Wagers earned his bachelor's degree in Food Science from the University of Illinois and an associate's degree in Culinary Arts and in Baking and Pastry Arts from Sullivan College, Louisville, Kentucky. He has worked for Hyatt, Grisanti's in Denver, and at the Bahnoff Buffet Bern in Bern, Switzerland, where he was a pastry chef responsible for supplying nine restaurants and banquet facilities with desserts. His specialties were sugar, chocolate and pastillage.

DAVID YEUNG, PH.D.

GENERAL MANAGER – GLOBAL NUTRITION, H.J. HEINZ COMPANY

Dr. David Yeung

Dr. Yeung has dedicated his life to helping people all over the world improve their nutrition including through the delicious recipes he has provided for this collection. Today, as General Manager – Global Nutrition, H.J. Heinz Company, he oversees extensive research into the possible health benefits of lycopene, a powerful antioxidant that is abundant in tomatoes. He is the co-author, with Venket Rao, Ph.D., of *Unlock the Power of Lycopene: REDefining Your Diet for Optimum Health.*

Dr. Yeung has established nutrition education programs in Australia, Canada, China, the Czech Republic, Hungary, India, Poland, Spain, Thailand, and Russia. He has served as consultant to the Food and Agriculture Organization, the Micronutrients Initiatives, and the U.S. Agency for International Development.

Dr. Yeung received his doctorate from the Department of Nutritional Sciences, Faculty of Medicine, University of Toronto, Canada. He was an associate professor in Applied Human Nutrition at the University of Guelph, Ontario before joining the H.J. Heinz Company of Canada. Remaining academically active, he is an Adjunct Professor in the Department of Nutritional Sciences, University of Toronto, and has been an adjunct and honorary professor in universities in Canada and the People's Republic of China. Dr. Yeung has published extensively in refereed scientific journals and has served on numerous scientific committees in Canada and the U.S.

In 1997, Dr. Yeung received the Earle Willard McHenry Award from the Canadian Society of Nutritional Sciences for distinguished service in nutrition.

RANIA L. HARRIS
CERTIFIED CHEF & OWNER – RANIA'S CATERING, MT. LEBANON, PA

Rania Harris is a certified chef, event coordinator, cooking school teacher, and local television and radio talent who began her catering business twenty four years ago from her Mt. Lebanon kitchen. Her goal was to cater "just a few" parties a year - to satisfy her love for cooking and entertaining. One party led to another and her business grew into a full-scale catering operation, as well as a gourmet take-out shop, cafe, cooking school, and pastry shop.

Rania L. Harris

Harris's natural sense of food presentation was enhanced by her studies with Master Pastry Chef Gunther Heiland and the Culinary Institute's Chef Timothy Ryan (formerly of La Normande). Her culinary career has included catering for Presidential candidates, senators, governors and several well-known Hollywood personalities. Throughout the years, her philosophy has remained simple and consistent: Treat each one of her clients and students as though they were guests in her own home...and never hold back on a recipe request!!!

Harris has served as a Heinz media spokesperson, including at the Heinz Tailgatin' Station at Heinz Field. For eight years, Harris had a regular cooking segment on WTAE-TV's weekend news. She has taught cooking segments on Pittsburgh's Talking, Evening Magazine, Hello Pittsburgh and Pittsburgh Today. She can now be seen on KDKA-TV2. She also has a regular cooking segment on KDKA radio with Larry Richert on Thursday mornings at 8:07 A.M.

Besides being heavily involved with the local culinary community, Harris was featured nationally in *Bon Appétit* (April 1985) as "an outstanding cooking school teacher."

INDEX

INDEX (CONTINUED)

Pastitso, 81
Sensational Sloppy Joes, 5
Shepherd's Pie, 53
Stuffed Tomatoes, 68

GROUND PORK
Pastitso, 81

GROUND TURKEY
Chili, 4
Heinz "TK" Tacoz, 101
Pasta di Genoa
with Turkey Meatballs, 57
Sensational Sloppy Joes, 5
Turkey Chili
with White Beans, 56
Turkey TD Burgers with
Barbecued Red Onions, 8

LASAGNA
Classic Two-Sauce Lasagna, 59
Hearty Meat Lasagna, 58
Mema's Lasagna, 60
Vegetarian Lasagna
Roll-Ups di Napoli, 116

MEATLESS ENTRÉES
Baked Pasta Ragu, 49
Classic Stuffed Shells, 79
Eggplant Parmigiana, 62
Sicilian Pasta, 76
Tortellini Primavera, 77

Tricolor Tortellini
with Spinach & Tomato in
Alfredo Sauce, 52
Vegetarian Lasagna
Roll-Ups di Napoli, 116

MUSHROOMS
Chicken Cacciatore, 64
Chili Italiano, 106
Tortellini Primavera, 77

MUSSELS
Mussels Marinara, 48

PANCAKES
Apple Pancakes
with Cider Sauce, 32

PASTA
Baked Pasta Ragu, 49
Chicken Cacciatore, 64
Chicken Noodle Casserole, 74
Chicken Parmesan, 78
Chili Italiano, 106
Classic Stuffed Shells, 79
Fried Ravioli with
Tomato Rosemary Sauce, 119
Layered Angel Hair
and Sausage Bake, 75
Minestrone
with Pesto Meatballs, 44
Pasta and Chicken
di Toscana, 71

Pasta di Genoa
with Turkey Meatballs, 57
Pastitso, 81
Pork Medallions Arrabbiata, 80
Sicilian Pasta, 76
Soup di Napoli, 46
Southwestern Pasta Salad, 10
Southwestern Tricolor
Tortellini Salad
with Balsamic Vinaigrette, 113
Tortellini Primavera, 77
Tricolor Tortellini
with Spinach & Tomato in
Alfredo Sauce, 52

PIES
Chocolate Angel Pie, 123
Jumbleberry Pie, 134
Love Apple Pie, 131
Sausage Spinach Pie, 70
Shepherd's Pie, 53

PINEAPPLE
Chicken Kickoff Kabobs, 19
EZ Marinader™
Grilled Chicken Breasts, 18
Fast Football Franks, 100
Grilled Vegetable Kabobs, 27
Honey 'N' Spice
Chicken Kabobs, 26
Sweet-and-Sour Chicken, 90

INDEX (CONTINUED)

MEASUREMENTS AND EQUIVALENTS

MEASUREMENTS	
Dash	= less than ⅛ tsp
1 Tbsp	= 3 tsp
2 Tbsp	= 1 oz
4 Tbsp	= ¼ cup
5⅓ Tbsp	= ⅓ cup
8 Tbsp	= ½ cup
16 Tbsp	= 1 cup
8 oz	= 1 cup
16 oz	= 1 lb
2 cups	= 1 lb/1 pint
2 pints	= 1 qt/4 cups
4 quarts	= 1 gallon

METRIC CONVERSION	
VOLUME	
1 tsp	= 5 ml
1 Tbsp	= 15 ml
2 Tbsp	= 30 ml
1 cup	= 240 ml
1 pint	= 480 ml
1 quart	= 960 ml

WEIGHT	
1 oz	= 28 gm
1 lb	= 454 gm
2.2 lbs	= 1 Kg (1,000 gm)